About the Author

 *Sfurti Sahare* is a dynamic motivational speaker known for her high-energy pep talks. Nagpur-born Sfurti completed her degree in computer engineering from Pune University and turned her attention to motivational speaking to inspire the young and the old alike, to make a difference in their lives. She loves enthralling large crowds with her carefully crafted inspirational programs. Sfurti works as a performance coach for various corporates, startups, athletes and entrepreneurs.

Her signature programs include:

- **Being World-class with Sfurti Sahare:** A program designed exclusively for those who want to build their own brand. Best suited for aspiring actors, cricketers, authors and entrepreneurs.

- **The Mastermind:** A full-day workshop on developing a superior mindset to understand how to deal with stress, mounting workload and new opportunities.

To know more about Sfurti's training programs,
visit **www.sfurtisahare.com** or
write to **team@sfurtisahare.com**.
You can also follow Sfurti on YouTube and Instagram.

Think

and

Win

like

Dhoni

**5
Success
Secrets**

Sfurti Sahare

JAICO PUBLISHING HOUSE

Ahmedabad Bangalore Bhopal Bhubaneswar Chennai
Delhi Hyderabad Kolkata Lucknow Mumbai

Published by Jaico Publishing House
A-2 Jash Chambers, 7-A Sir Phirozshah Mehta Road
Fort, Mumbai - 400 001
jaicopub@jaicobooks.com
www.jaicobooks.com

THINK AND WIN LIKE DHONI
ISBN 978-81-8495-890-4

First Jaico Impression: 2016
Ninth Jaico Impression: 2017

Page design and layout: Jojy Philip, Delhi

Printed by
Snehesh Printers
320-A, Shah & Nahar Ind. Est. A-1
Lower Parel, Mumbai - 400 013

Contents

Foreword

MS Dhoni is a boy who emerged from the narrow alleys of Ranchi and made his mark nationally and internationally probably in the shortest span of his cricketing career. As a person who has observed Dhoni's innings for so long, I believe his greatest strength is his ability to stay calm in all possible situations. Following his lead, I have also started to stay calm. I have observed that being calm and composed not only helps you to take sound, positive decisions, but it also augments your intuitive power. I feel this is one of the main reasons behind Dhoni's extraordinary alertness during the crucial phases of a match.

Also, he is quicker in understanding a delivery when compared to other players. I believe that while batting, he can spot a ball a fraction of a second earlier, which gives him an advantage even when he's not technically correct.

This is a very rare quality because to do so, you need to concentrate, you need to be in the present moment.

Think and Win Like Dhoni is a boon to those who want to win; to those who want to work and achieve more in life. This book will expand one's horizon, vision and self-belief.

Do read, enjoy and share.

All the best to Sfurti.

Maninder Singh
Former cricketer

Acknowledgements

I was barely 11 years old when Dada (Sourav Ganguly) introduced me to the colossal world of cricket. He taught me to believe in my dreams and showed me that impossible is just another word. Thank you, Dada.

At 18, I moved to Pune to study computer engineering, but my first love, cricket, couldn't stay away.

Then at 21, it was Mahi (MS Dhoni) sir's World Cup-winning shot that generated the curiosity in me to know more about the sport. My heartfelt thanks to Mr. Muhammed Wasim (Mahi sir's childhood friend) who introduced me to MSD and shared many stories about him.

From being an engineer to writing a book was not as easy as I thought. It was my coach Mr. Bhupendra Singh Rathore who continuously motivated me and told me, "Sfurti, you can do it." Those priceless words have helped me go on during crucial moments.

I would like to thank Ms. Devasmita Dey Chowdury for helping me edit the manuscript when the book was not a book but just a word document. I wish her all the very best for her upcoming projects. I would like to thank Mr. Buddhadev Ghosh, Sports Editor, Tara TV, Kolkata. I am also thankful to Rhiti Sports for all their help and special thanks to Anuj Bahri for getting me the right publisher. It was great working with you, sir.

I am truly grateful to my Mom (Manda Sahare) who has travelled with me to Ranchi and put up with my mood swings. I am also thankful to my Dad (D.C. Sahare) from whom I have inherited the spirit of 'thinking big and beyond' and how can I forget my little bro (Piyush) who told me, "Nuso, just keep going. Don't think about money, don't think about people. It's your life, live your way."

Why This Book?

My name is Sfurti. I come from Nagpur and I am a software engineer. And that's not all. Here is the highlight of my introduction:

I met MS Dhoni!

Now before we argue that fans do make that effort to meet their idols, which does not necessarily need to turn into a book, I will tell you what this is all about. This book is about an extraordinary journey made by an ordinary girl that turned out to be a life-altering phenomenon. But does that qualify me to write a book about him? Maybe it does, or maybe my quest to unravel a few things about him that were making the rounds those days, qualifies a read.

The story is worth telling, for I am itching to share it. And it's worth listening to, for it changed me forever.

It all started way back when I was in my second year of engineering. Barely 20-years-old, I was watching an

Indian Premier League (IPL) match with my gang of friends in a coffee shop and a discussion about Dhoni ensued. Throughout the 'Coffee with Cricket' discussion I felt that this 'luck' word was given more importance than it deserved. Something was not right about it. By then, Dhoni had just scored 16 runs in the last over. It was a match against Kings XI Punjab (2010) in Dharamsala and Captain Cool took Chennai Super Kings to semi-finals with a brilliant 54*(not out) runs from 29 deliveries.

That was just one such, among the many that I can illustrate where Dhoni has performed, captained under heavy pressure and won us the game. Just think of the ICC World Cup Final 2011 or the decision to give the final over to Joginder Sharma in ICC World Twenty20 against Pakistan in 2007.

He had been hailed as the uncrowned prince of the cricketing world and people, left, right and centre proclaimed him as 'lucky'.

And that his 'luck' would steer Indian cricket to great heights.

That his 'luck' would bring home the World Cup Trophy that year.

Media called him, 'the lucky dude with flowing hair'.

Girls cooed a 'luck charm' of the team and batted their eyelids Minnie Mouse style!

But I thought we were missing something. What was it?

We were, of course, missing the point! The point of learning from a living phenomenon – **The Art of Winning**.

He is hailed as the best Player under Pressure in the world. He led India to the cup in the World Twenty20 in 2007. He, along with his boys, brought home the World Cup in 2011, besides also gifting us the ICC Champions Trophy in 2013, donning the captain's hat.

With him as their captain, the Chennai Super Kings have won two titles and qualified six times in the IPL Finals in eight seasons so far from 2008 to 2015.

I refused to dismiss this whole Dhoni turbulence as just an act of 'luck'. There has to be more. The media was calling him the 'Champion of the Era'.

I wanted to know what made him so special.

You ask me why?

Because luck alone cannot take you so far. What takes you so far is what Dhoni has got in him. I believe that knowing it and sharing it can be a winning factor in everyone's life.

So for those who are inquisitive to learn the Dhoni-way and his success mantra, read on, because I have spent three long years researching him.

No kidding.

The first I chanced upon Dhoni was during his net practice in 2005, when he played domestic cricket. It was in Nagpur, my hometown and, I was in my 9th Standard. And here I was standing beholding my idol with long flowing hair, quiet in disposition, as he jogged around the field with the ball in his hand. I saw him throw the ball, catch it and bounce it as he played along the field. He was then a 'nobody' in the gang of celebs.

In the years to come, I watched all his matches on TV. I followed all his interviews. I like to watch the way he handles reporters and their provocative questions. I studied his body language on and off the field. I kept an ear for the words that came out from the dressing room, from his peers' POV from the commentary box, his after match presentation interviews, his steady fast eyes, assured smile – everything. When I was satisfied that now I know almost about all that is out there to know about Dhoni, I finally made the journey to meet him, to see what, being in his vicinity, actually felt like.

And lo! It felt like I have stepped in an unseen whirlpool of power and energy. I got mesmerized by his simplicity, the easy, relaxed way of talking, and the 'no air' attitude. He smiled a lot when we spoke. His smile is unreserved and he does not do it for the sake of cameras. When I told him that I had just about started with the book, he promptly assured me that, *"**And you will finish it soon enough. Don't worry. Follow your heart and follow the process.**"* The way he delivered those simple words of encouragement said a lot about the natural leader in him. I wondered how exactly he manages to concoct this heady mix. Interacting with him made me tinkle with excitement.

I have observed that while Dhoni leads his entire self to the field, one could almost see the invisible signals of a winner's lessons that he shoots along the way. The power trail he leaves behind is undeniable.

In my journey to discover Dhoni, I have picked up his

five traits that make him a winner of such magnitude – five undeniable traits of his power trail.

Just 5.
They are simple.
They are achievable.
They are within us, to dig-up and use.

Through the length of this book I will bring forth these very 5 traits that have altered Dhoni's life and you will find that the man himself tells you that it can alter your life too.

All I would say, before I get started is that – *Try toh karo!* (Just Try.) It's not all that tough.

I vividly remember the day I was watching Celkon Mobile Cup Final 2013 against Sri Lanka. Dhoni was in the crease, 15 runs required of 6 balls with 9 wickets down. Dhoni delivered under pressure to clinch the Final Cup. India won the game by 1 wicket with 2 balls remaining.

(IND-203/9 in 49.4 overs, Sri Lanka- 201/10 48.5, Dhoni scored 45 runs off 52 balls)

On the TV screen, I see his set, icy cold face devoid of any expression. I am biting my nails and rocking my legs in an undignified manner. The commentator in the commentary box goes easy and low. The crowd breathes a single heavy breath and a gust of hot dusty air blows through and settles. But Dhoni is completely calm.

It made me wonder. "How come I am biting my nails and he isn't? What's he thinking? What's behind that set face and that pair of calm eyes?"

There were too many questions chasing one another in my mind. But if I was looking for my answer in Dhoni's eyes and his body language, I wasn't getting any. He did not quiver. He did not give away his state of mind. He did not shuffle his feet or bite his nails. If he was nervous, there was no way of knowing. And like me, even the opponents were clueless. Reading his psyche to plan out a combat move was not to be.

What did that mean?

It meant that if there was a set game plan that was followed so far by the cricketing fraternity, Dhoni subtly but surely was changing those very rules.

So then what is the Dhoni factor?

What makes an ordinary person like him rise to such extraordinary heights? What can we learn from Dhoni that will make us reach our peak?

I went and met Dada.

I knew that not only did Sourav Ganguly captain Dhoni, he was the one who identified the winner in him much before he was identified by the world at large.

It was Ganguly who promoted Dhoni up in the order against Pakistan and he went on to smash 148 runs. So there could be no better person other than Ganguly who could give me a perspective about Dhoni. I wanted to ask him what he saw in Dhoni. What is it that made him bet on Dhoni? I also wanted to meet my idol, Ganguly, with whom I had once won the "Sourav Ke Saath Dinner" contest back in 2004 at Nagpur, when I was barely in my teens, but knew him enough to be crazy about him!

Ganguly's insight about Dhoni changed the course of the book for good. He did not talk to me about Dhoni's cricketing skills. He did not tell me how well he trained himself or how hard he hit that ball. Instead he spoke about Dhoni's immense mental skills. He said that,

> *"His mental programming is the key. It's his mind that is the differentiating factor between being successful and being a winner."*

What is this 'Mental Programming'?

Ganguly further added that becoming successful depends upon lots of things, like talent, training, help, backing, etc. But winning depends on only one thing – a mind to win. That mind is an attitude. It's a killer trait. And to be a winner, you have to possess that.

And Dhoni has that trait that makes him a winner.

I also spoke to Debashish Dutta, a veteran sports journalist for the last 34 years, who is currently associated with *Aajkal* Kolkata and *Mid-Day* in Mumbai. Mr Dutta said,

> *"Dhoni is different from others. He is different from you and me. His mind works in a different way and that 'way' is the winner's way."*

The scribe also said that the thing to understand about Dhoni is that it's not just his positive attitude that makes him a winner. It's the complete annihilation of everything negative that makes him what he is today. The greatness factor in him cannot be denied or ignored.

While these questions raced in my mind, I found myself pondering over a few more things. I tried finding answers to questions of life – the Dhoni way.

For example, let's look at the way in which Shah Rukh Khan, who was a nobody in the film industry, became a Bollywood icon. He didn't have a godfather in the industry and he is not particularly handsome, tall, or fair. He has achieved something many star kids with heavy backing couldn't. That's pretty much the Dhoni style.

Mark Zuckerberg, the co-founder and CEO of the social networking site Facebook, dropped out of college to start his company. Today he is the fourth richest person in the world and the youngest billionaire while many brilliant 'A' graders fail to make it big in life.

Or take the case of some of the cricketing legends' kids who fail to shine despite the fact that they have everything given to them in a silver platter.

Dhoni, who had almost everything against him, manages to swim against the tide and win the world. How does he do that?

Also, in the sport of cricket, is it possible for two international teams, standing side by side in the same filed, to have such varied sustainability? Pakistan's cricket team, whose victory score with India is more, has never won a match in the World Cup against India. Why can't a seasoned team like Pakistan handle the pressure of a World Cup match against India? What happens to them on the field?

Leading psychologists attribute this phenomenon to mental skills. They say that

> *Around 70% credit goes to mental skills in the path to success. The rest 30% is talent born-with and acquired.*

While media makes red of just the obvious 30%, I was digging into the larger 70%, for that's what makes the 30% usable. The answer was Dhoni and his immense psychological scope. Now listen to this story and see if you can grasp the mental frame of Dhoni. While writing this book, I interviewed many people. Laxmi Ratan Shukla was one of them. You may wonder why *him*? The answer to that is simple: Shukla shared the field with Dhoni when the latter was just Dhoni and not 'The Dhoni'. Shukla played the Ranji Trophy, Duleep Trophy and other domestic matches with him and captained him too. Their togetherness in cricket goes back to 1999 when Dhoni's long, sexy hair had turned the heads of boys and girls alike. I asked Shukla if he would like to comment on the moment when India won the Cup in 2011 and the captain left the ground without much fanfare.

Shukla said, "See, this is what we need to understand

about Dhoni if we are trying to study his mind. Only a person like Dhoni can do this; Win such a mammoth match and then hand over the laurels to someone else and quietly retreat. When Dhoni was asked to comment on this, he had said that this win belongs to Sachin Tendulkar. Dhoni is unparalleled because he alone is capable of such things. If we can understand this element in him, we can decode the winning factor in Dhoni."

So I wanted to decode it. I wanted to know how he viewed winning and losing; His approach towards cricket; His opinions about his peers; His attitude towards his team.

I wanted to know the great Dhoni factor.

And those factors were the five Dhoni-traits that served the answers.

Media splashes a lot about his powerful muscles. He is known as a hard hitter. It's sexy to view those sinews work for fours and sixes that makes the crowd roar in excitement.

It's so picture perfect.

While much is said about his abilities on the field, not much is elaborated about his mental skills beyond the general observation that he is a calm person. But interestingly, when asked, Dhoni over and again attributed Team India's victory to skills other than the ones widely talked about. Even more interesting is the fact that no one paid much attention. Neither did media give much mileage when he talked about the importance of mind-power in the process of winning. Through him I have learnt that **if one**

can control his mind, he can control much of anything in the universe.

In the recent match between India and Bangladesh that qualified as a nail biting finish match, Bangladesh had to make 2 runs from 3 balls. But the batsman was run out by the wicket keeper and skipper Dhoni. It was a tense moment for everyone – the players of both the teams, fans of both the countries as well as all cricket lovers across board. Why this run out by Dhoni got analysed on so many counts is that the way he conducted it. Dhoni had removed his gloves to ensure better grip on the ball. He positioned himself cool and calm, and when the ball came to him, he actually ran towards the stumps. He did not throw the ball from where he caught it, but believed that he could actually outrun the batsman and cut him down. Fans witnessed not just a power packed finish but also the work of a cool mind that is devoid of obsession. Since he doesn't obsess about his decision, he doesn't get into a frenzy in such tight corners, and neither does he panic. I believe this attitude of his should be a bonus takeaway along with the win of the day!

While we give much time and effort in going to the gym to build our muscles, we conveniently ignore the muscles of our brain. Our mind too needs some nurturing. It's exactly these muscles that Dhoni brings to the foray when he plays the game. It's all of these five magical traits that he walks with, when he walks into the field – the muscles of his brain and its immense powers.

So, let's talk about these five traits of Dhoni and see if it sounds like the mind of a winner!

These traits are simple yet loaded with results that have the power to enhance your productivity a hundred folds.

Try toh karo!

How to read this book?

1. Proceed chapter-wise. The pages will unfold in a manner that they will help open up your mind to a journey within.

2. Share every Dhoni principle with at least two people on the same day. It will help you absorb the concept almost instantly. My team has designed the flow with the help of renowned sports psychologist Dr. Biswajit Bam who has worked with the likes of Sachin Tendulkar and Rahul Dravid for a long time. So please trust us on this.

3. Keep this *'Try toh karo!'* in your pocket. It has been used several times in the book for a reason.

So keep your hopes high, fasten your faith belt and dare to believe in your dreams. Because this book is an attempt to help you make your dream come true, the Dhoni way!

The Right Attitude

Not very long ago, Dhoni was in his newly-acquired Land Rover, travelling from Delhi to Jaipur via NH 8. His friend was behind the wheels, speeding up that beast. Now, getting to gear up your accelerator on such a smooth stretch is just a call of the moment. The two of them were having a blast when suddenly, from nowhere, a car appeared in front of them. The Land Rover screeched to a halt. It was a close shave. His friend held his breathe in anticipation of a rebuff, but Dhoni, his usual composed self, said,

> *"When life is running so smoothly why would you want to complicate things? You have a good family, good business and everything good going for you. Anything happening here would bring in the media, police and create unnecessary chaos. Take it easy man!"*

Years later, revisiting this memory, the friend said that the only stabilizing factor in that heart-in-the-mouth moment was Dhoni, who did not flinch an inch and smoothly brought things into perspective. "If we checked his pulse rate then," he told me, as he laughed remembering, "it would have read absolutely normal."

Now listen to this,

> *"Nobody has seen 'form'. It's a state of mind where you are confident and you think very positively."*

Dhoni had brilliantly quipped when he was asked to comment on the present 'in-form' players in the team. In this statement, he not only gives a different perspective to the idea of 'in-form', he also steers clear from making any negative statements to the media about his teammates. Experts reveal that there is a fresh approach to everything that Dhoni touches. For decades the cricketing world has used the 'in-form' and 'out-of-form' expressions. But Dhoni dismissed it in a jiffy with a new outlook. Suddenly those old expressions don't sound so smart anymore. Come to think of it, the ability to dent into such age-old, set ideas needs a certain degree of courage and Dhoni is known for it.

Evidently enough from the above pages, attitude is all about the 70-30 balance. At this point it would be great to establish that oft-heard saying about attitude that it's something someone is born with is all a nasty myth.

Attitude is something Dhoni has acquired with time, awareness, and conviction. People are born with some but they accumulate the rest on the way upwards in life.

When I sat down to write this chapter, I wanted to make sure that I can give my readers a definitive connection between all the attitude categories, what they exactly mean, and how these acted as the fulcrum in Dhoni's success.

Time and again we have all realized that winners think differently and do things differently. This chapter will focus on decoding our favourite captain's thought process and understand his attitude towards cricket and life. We will try and unravel the winning secrets of Dhoni that make him an achiever of this magnitude.

Unceasingly Positive

Narratives of positivity always inspire us. A small recap of Dhoni's background, from his humble beginnings to his subsequent iconic rise in the cricketing world, will bring forth his exemplary positive attitude.

Now spare some time to comprehend this:

Hailing from a small town Ranchi, which he has by now successfully pinned it on the world map – had nothing much in terms of cricket, or recognition. When one could hardly find cricketing gear in Ranchi, let alone good playing grounds or commendable coaching institutes, where boys even had to do with canvas balls, Dhoni refused to give up and did it, and how!

Visiting Ranchi, I found it lacking in the sheen and facilities of a big city. It was then I realized what set Dhoni apart from all and sundry like myself. While I, hailing from a big city, crib for things I don't have or things I can't facilitate, Dhoni doesn't. He has that flair for turning his limitations into positive streaks simply by not letting them stand in his way.

We will take a few instances from the sport that made him to drive home the importance of positive attitude as a way to success – like the things that he usually says, things his friends, teammates, and coaches say about him, the way he behaves, etc.

> *"I believe in seeing the positive side of the story. For me it was a time to rest and watch a lot of TV. Spend time with my family and friends and play with my dog."*

This was Dhoni's comment after missing out on the Asia Cup 2014 owing to an injury.

That for me is a vibe so extraordinary that it's hard to ignore, for here was a man, who would soon be synonymous with calmness, quickly calculating the utter pointlessness of being depressed and pondering on something he had no control over.

For the captain of Team India, it should have been a matter of great anxiety to miss a tournament, but that didn't make him lose practicality. He was injured and could not play, so he instead chose to make the best of the situation.

> *"It's not what happens to you. It's how you react to it!*

During his initial days of playing the Ranji Trophy, Dhoni was down with jaundice just before the tournament. Making things worse, his hand too was injured on the field.

A visibly worried Keshav Ranjan Banerjee, his first coach, asked Dhoni, "What next?"

The eternally calm Dhoni had simply stated the facts – jaundice and injury together was an impossible situation, therefore, he couldn't play.

Hopeful of Dhoni's big break, the news came as a disappointment to Banerjee. He perceived it as an opportunity lost due to unavoidable reasons. But Dhoni, his usual calm self, was quick to brush it off saying, *"Koi nahi. Phir* chance *aaiega."* (I will get a chance again, don't worry.)

Years later while Banerjee narrated the incident to me, his face seemed as perplexed as it had been with his student's calm approach towards this depressing situation then. Banerjee feared that the incident would break Dhoni and he would soon join the league of those promising players (who Banerjee coached throughout the years), who gave up when faced with hurdles. But, Dhoni never nursed a weak heart. He took things in his stride, overcame obstacles, and went on to win hearts.

Psychology would tell you nothing different. The situation is same for all, but reactions differ. This is the major difference between a performer and a non-performer.

After having observed him for quite some time now, I find myself following a very simple exercise that has helped me a lot personally and I suggest you try it too. Whenever I come across a challenging situation,

I ask myself how would have Dhoni reacted to this? It makes things simpler for me and puts things into perspective.

Think like Dhoni.

People are thrown into different situations from day one of their lives. When we play, we learn to handle competition. We work, we earn money, and we dream dreams and follow them. We develop ambitions, identify a goal. We pick up hobbies for fun, struggle for jobs, fight for success, rejoice in victory and sulk in failure.

I started following a simple practice, how would have MSD reacted to this situation' instead.

In all these phases, there's one defining point that underlines the entire journey of life and that is **The Big 'A' – Attitude.** Mind makes a man and precisely for that reason the mind has to be trained to form strong, fortified scaffolding around your persona, talent, dream, aspiration, and passion. Life will climb up this scaffolding, the one which will define us. That scaffolding which defines us is what we call "Attitude".

> **"Success is all about conditioning your mind."**
> —MS DHONI

After winning the first match against Pakistan in the last World Cup, Dhoni had said:

> *"We need to stay happy, stay positive all the time and approach each match with the right frame of mind."*

In his numerous interviews you must have heard Dhoni often say that,

> *Winning is a great morale booster for the team and it will help them perform better. The same man, when he loses a match, without dismissing them makes it a point to say that he has learnt from the loss and that's why losing was sometimes great too.*

Breathing positivity in almost every comment, Dhoni quips at ease when questioned about a fielder who dropped too many catches, or brushes off saying, "it was not his day today", when quizzed about a bowler giving away too many runs. When asked what discussion ensued in the green room after a particular bowler delivered badly, he said, "We just left him alone. He will sort out things himself. He's a professional player. He does not need to be schooled." This killer trait sets him apart from everyone. Dhoni moulds situations in his favour and forever looks at the positive side of things.

But how's it practically possible for a man to be so composed?

Because Dhoni knows it only too well that negative thoughts can only breed doubts. Doubt is a negative attitude which has negative power, and takes you away from your goal and from the object of your passion.

> "Success is 99% attitude and 1% aptitude."
> —CELESTINE CHUA

While cricket gurus are often heard churning out how the game is primarily about talent, Dhoni has proven it time and again how it is actually all about attitude. With the right attitude in place, talent can be acquired and Dhoni has established to the world that **attitude comes before talent.**

Dhoni's life has had traces of cynicisms too. There has been a saying that Dhoni is not always technically correct. Now, what could that mean?

Obviously this statement holds a lot of significance and once again takes us back to the gullies that used to be the first field for Dhoni. The unchaperoned and untutored cricket that he played in the gullies of Ranchi still reflects in his organized cricket. When a rookie gets into the game, there are many technicalities and fine tuning that he goes through – from learning to hold a bat correctly, knowing the perfect angle to swing it at, and also synchronising your shoulders to get the maximum effect while spinning that ball. Experts feel that these are the technicalities Dhoni lacks. But Dhoni rises above all these and his attitude comes clean as a winner on the field.

> *"If it is important to you, you will find a way. If not, you will find an excuse."*

Hard Work Dhoni Style

"If you practice a shot 100 times, only then you will be confident about it. That confidence will give you positive attitude. Confidence without hard work is fake confidence. Failure is sure to happen. Go full throttle. I completely believe in it."

—MS DHONI

Mohhammed Wasim recollected one of his fondest memories about Dhoni and I sharpened my ears. I won't call it revolutionary as far as insights go, but goes a long way in understanding the character of a person.

It was just another gully match at Ranchi and our captain was quite young. Wasim fondly remembered how they played into teams and rode their bikes all the way to the big playground on the day of a tournament. Wasim was playing in the rival team and just a night before the match, Dhoni had said, "Do whatever you want Wasim *bhai*. My team will win."

"That's not happening," Wasim told him. "My team has the best bowlers and batsmen."

"Maybe, I don't know," Dhoni said, "but my team knows how to win."

"The next day we were supposed to be on the ground by 3 PM. Amir (Dhoni's another childhood friend with long flowing hair, which MSD didn't liked initially) went to MSD's home as they would ride to the ground together. But his father told Amir that Dhoni left home with his bat at 11 AM. When Amir reached the grounds, he found a meticulous Dhoni in the nets, practising. It was just another gully game, but Dhoni had to win it still. There was no two ways about it.

For him it was never the question of a big or a small match, the only thing that mattered was winning.

It was an attitude brimming with confidence.

Come hell or high water, it was difficult to keep him off the field, or so coach Banerjee tells me. When it rained and it kept them off cricket, Dhoni would play football. And if for some reason that didn't work out, he played tennis. During an ankle injury, he sat on his chair throwing darts. No matter how hard the situation presented itself, there was nothing stopping him. He likes to floor the accelerator and go full throttle, as he believes if you go full throttle on the job at hand, you can achieve confidence.

Sourav Ganguly too voiced the same opinion when I requested him to give me a talk on confidence for my readers. He asserted that confidence is something that comes from within, but there is definitely a way to do it. "Take one step at a time and polish it. A small achievement will give you the necessary adrenaline shot in the arm to take the next step. The next step will always be better than the first one, because by now you are loaded with some confidence. And that's how you build on it. Deep down, you have to develop it with self-belief," remarked our dearest *Dada*. Saying that, he leaned forward, pointed a finger at me and said,

> *"Sfurti-with-confidence and Sfurti-without-confidence are two different personalities."*

Dhoni is that robust person who knows to give it all. He was always the first person to enter the field during a practice session and the last one to leave in his younger days.

While we have all heard a lot about hard work, it's through Dhoni that I learnt that hard work too has a process. The donkey-style slogging will not necessarily bring in the desired result. In a fast-track world where surviving means shoulder-cracking with the best, hard work needs a scaffolding of strong mental skills (elaborated in Chapter 3). So, as you go over the chapter, please do link the concept with hard work and you will get a fair idea of it, the Dhoni style, which is result-oriented.

While Dhoni has played more domestic cricket, international-level players still came as a test to him. After one such game he said, "Playing at the domestic level, you cannot prepare yourself for bowlers like Anil Kumble and Harbhajan Singh. No domestic bowler can match the pace they bowl at."

He was no stranger to the fact that there was more hard work to be done and he didn't take anything for granted. He never stopped preparing himself. Aware of the bigwigs in cricket, he got into the roll, making himself stronger and more skilful in the game. Mastering the art of cricket, he infused his own innovations into it. As a result, we have the 'helicopter shot' that left every bowler devastated. The sheer unorthodox way of handling the willow, invented by Dhoni, made that his Masterstroke.

There is no short cut to success and you cannot skip **hard work** or fool your system. It is irreplaceable and the formula, omnipresent.

To make your mark in the world, to emerge a champion, the formula needs to be followed.

For people with inborn talent, the learning part becomes a matter of temperament. While some are born with talents, others tend to acquire them along the way.

As our very own Ganguly always says,

> **"It's not talent that makes a winner. It's what you do with the talent that matters."**

Now, Dhoni has got that talent and what actually makes him emerge a winner in every situation, whether tough or trivial, is his hard work and the right attitude. But what actually gives him an edge over the others is his two distinctive character streaks – fearlessness and calmness.

A Fearless Fighter

> *That fearlessness is not just the talk-of-the-town, but talk-of-the-world.*

Let's take this scenario:

It was the summer of 2005, an April to remember. Pakistan was on a cricketing tour of India. Dhoni was on the field playing his 5th match and 2nd series. Sourav Ganguly, the then captain of the Indian Team pulled Dhoni from his usual 6th position to the 3rd. Dhoni was instructed to just go and hit the ball. A composed Dhoni let his bat speak fiercely and had a good knock scoring 148 from just 123 deliveries. If we replay his brilliant knock and observe carefully, we will find that he had managed to hit the ball in all directions. There was not a single shot that he did not try, and not a single point on the field that he left untouched. The commentators went gaga over his 'unorthodox' shots and the 'different style' that Dhoni embodied, leaving everyone impressed.

Now, let us use this as a case-in-point to understand Dhoni's attitude, because much later, in a media event, Ganguly recalled this very match and a few more, when he commented:

> **"The greatest quality of Mahi is that whenever he is given an opportunity, he performs."**

So let's take a look at the pressure points:

He is a newcomer.

That was his second series against Pakistan, while in his very first against Bangladesh he could not score, even ducking in the first match.

Pressure was mounting on him to keep his position as a wicket-keeper.

To top that, Ganguly had asked him to go first-down.

When *Dada* asked Dhoni to make his entry, the team had just lost the Little Master as he fell short of time running and had to go back with a 2. The Pakistani bowlers, brimming with confidence, were bowling at a certain line and rhythm, very set, knowing the strength of their bowling side. Dhoni's task was to get cracking on the bowlers and that's exactly what he did.

In this situation, when the Virendra Sehwag-Sachin Tendulkar partnership died a quick death, Dhoni managed to score a 148, an effort that only transpired because of his fearlessness. He left all negativity and pressure at the dressing room and did his best.

- *"Will I be able to face the Pakistani bowling attack which is lethal?"*
- *"Will I lose Team India if I fail to perform?"*
- *"What will the media say?"*
- *"What will my friends say?"*
- *"If I fail now, I will never get a second chance."*
- *"This will be the end. Oh! What a shame! How embarrassing!"*

All these thoughts will come naturally to a player when a lot depends on him and he is fully aware of the situation. Dhoni's performance that was to decide his future in the team also mattered to him, and therefore, he had to deal with this thought process. He had to eliminate fear. Fear would have paralyzed him.

In the beginning we talked about Dhoni's luck factor. But is right to attribute his successes to his luck because he was given an opportunity and he could make the best of it? Is everyone able to make the best use of given opportunities? Is everybody able to eliminate all the psychological hooks, and push ahead? Can everybody keep their fears aside the way Dhoni does? A person who can do it is a winner, and we still just call him lucky, so what do we call the rest? Losers?

Commentator Harsha Bhogle once said,

"Dhoni's greatest strength is his fearlessness."

He was given an opportunity. He used it to the fullest.

While all kinds of attitude have been discussed, 'fear' has never been categorized in the attitude category. But, **fear is an attitude.** We have often labelled people around us as 'fearful' or 'courageous'. A fearful person puts hurdles all the way to his goal. A fearless one just sees the goal and goes head on to achieve it. The fearless too have to go past the hurdles, but he doesn't stop; he tackles them on the way with the right frame of mind. Recognizing the presence of fear and trying to overcome it will be the first step towards achieving such desired results.

So what are those obstacles that get in the way of our success? According to Dhoni, fear is just an illusion of the mind, which doesn't exist in reality.

The more you entertain fear, the more you will attract it in your life. It will sit between you and your target, the size of Mount Everest. Some people fear the escalator or the elevator, while others are fearful of water. A corporate guy will fear a decision backlash while a businessman will lose sleep for nights on end over a multi-crore business deal. But fear does not have feet to stand on. It's a condition of your mind and your constant feeding it will make it larger than your life, your goal, and your destiny.

It's not just heights or water or a speed boat that people fear. People fear failure. That constant "What if I can't?" or that fear of change,"It means, I will have to leave home," or the fear of insignificance, "What if nobody gives a damn?" and of course, the fear of imperfection, "Everybody will see what an amateur I am," will always bug an insecure mind.

Too many people lose sleep prior to an important event – like a big meeting, a big show, an important business decision, or a match. We all know that and we think it is natural.

But what's the secret behind Dhoni's fearless self?

Before his debut match when asked if he could relax and sleep, he laughed and said that he indeed slept well. *"I had to be fresh for the next day."*

This is where presence of mind and calculation play major roles. Dhoni was farsighted enough to realize a no-sleep night would mean a mediocre performance. He does things to relax his mind and get that very essential sleep which will help him perform the next day.

How does Dhoni get a handle on fear?

Overcoming fears does not mean ignoring them or not acknowledging their presence. It means to take into account that this element of fear, at a given moment, is natural and so it exists – like a penalty shot or the last two balls of the match that would decide a win.

So how do you deal with it?

"The first step is to acknowledge it," Dhoni says. That dealt with, we need to do a little exercise: we need to mentally shove it into a box, close the lid tight, and keep it aside. This exercise will help us deal with it objectively which will be easier than fighting it. If we box that fear, it will automatically bring our strength and confidence to the forefront, because that fear which was occupying the mind space has been boxed and kept away. Taking the plunge, if you are a bungee jumper, or kicking that penalty shot, or hitting the six to win the match will become easier.

Captain Cool

Dhoni's second distinguishing strength is his calmness. On field his cool and calm body language is something that has been extensively talked about. Many a time, his calm attitude has turned the match around and made the team win.

"The team has been led by MS Dhoni's attitude. Most other sides can't do it because under such pressure, you lose your cool, the decision-making becomes cluttered and you lose your way. Because MSD is so adept at soaking in the pressure, we have done well in those situations."

—Former Team India Coach DUNCAN FLETCHER

> "His extraordinary calm attitude gives him immense mind space to use his conscious and sub-conscious mind effectively."
>
> — RAVI SHASTRI, Team Director & ex-player of the Indian Cricket Team

The entire world is reeling under the overpowering effect of Dhoni's **calm demeanour.** There was a time when bloodshot eyes, mercurial temperament and ready-to-shoot-at-the-drop-of-the hat attitude qualified as fitting for 'men'. Anything less fell under the donkey category. Men, if they didn't roar, were not 'good enough' to be called men!

Then came Dhoni and everyone was thrown off-guard.

Former Indian team coach Duncan Fletcher feels Dhoni's calm and composed attitude has enabled the team win three ICC events – the 2011 World Cup, the World Twenty20 in 2007, and the Champions Trophy 2013.

Dhoni is considered God when it comes to **dealing with**

> "One-day cricket is all about handling extreme pressure, especially when the side is down; understanding where the game is poised at that stage and finding your way out of that situation to end up on the winning side. Our excellent record when chasing totals shows that, and Dhoni right now, is the man of the hour."
>
> —DUNCAN FLETCHER

pressure. Often the opponents are at loss unable to handle a man who is so poised at any given point and can never be provoked. Nothing seems to ruffle him. No challenge is too big for him. No bowler is too strong for him. 'I am here, and I will do it' is forever engraved on his persona. And is anyone thinking of getting him nervous? Well, he doesn't seem to have nerves at all! They are all steel!

With the advent of a phenomenon like Dhoni, the world realized for the first time that the breed of 'angry young men' is obsolete. They do not stand a chance in these changing times where mind games and mental skill rule supreme. Cool, calm, and poised are the adjectives ruling the virtual world. While roaring takes you only so far, calmness takes you to limitless heights. It gives you superiority over everything else.

But what is Dhoni's covert calm mechanism?

Dhoni simply has a different take on things and what differs greatly is his Point of View (POV). So, when do we often lose our calm state of mind? It's when the pressure bogs us down. We lose the ability to think, let alone act.

> *Dhoni turns the table by viewing pressure as a given opportunity to prove his merit and become a hero.*

The POV instantly elevates the mind and puts him on the winning track.

Bowlers literally get on the batsman's nerves with all that show of aggressive body language, but these pressure tactics fail in front of a passive and determined Dhoni. He is impenetrable. With the mind game throttled, they are just left with a ball to throw. Dhoni is then able to make use of the opportunity to pave his way towards success.

In his words:

"When I bat, I just see the ball. It doesn't matter who is throwing it at me."

Captains on field take erratic decisions in tight situations, there by losing the game. But time and again it has been proved that such situations only serve to bring out the best in Dhoni. And hence he wears the crown of 'The Best Finisher.'

"The coolest man in world cricket MS Dhoni delivers when it most matters!"
—MICHAEL VAUGHAN, former English cricketer.

It is this outlook that has led him to take the Australians head on. The Aussies, famous, or more appropriately infamous for roughing up the opponents in the field, often resort to sledging. Not an alien term in the world of cricket, this technique is commonly used by players to weaken their opposition.

We are also not strangers to players making nasty eye

contacts, just to make them lose their calm and go weak on their knees.

During the match of 2005 against Pakistan, Shahid Afridi provoked Dhoni twice on the field so as to make Dhoni lose his cool. This is a part of the mind game often practised in cricket. Even though players are acclimatized with it, new players are not always immune to sledging. But Dhoni simply smiled and ignored Afridi and later went on to score 148 runs, paving the way to victory. India won. That 148 knock affixed his spot in the team.

You would love to emulate his secret to success as the captain. But his cool demeanour is a skill that needs nurturing and has to develop over time rather than followed in a jiffy.

"I wasn't so calm at a young age. I don't like to lose, so when I was young, I had trouble controlling my emotions. But, soon I realized that aggression is a waste of time and energy. Then I consciously practiced calmness and over a period of time, I learned to control my aggression."

The leader that he is he keeps his nerves on a tight leash and suggests strategies to his bowlers instead of losing his cool, yelling at them and miscalculating. As one who was born to rule and be the best at his job, he never flinches from motivating his boys to give their 100%, which is the prime quality of a captain.

His teammates are in awe of his persona. As the dressing room prattle suggests, even a mammoth score from the opponent fails to make him cringe. Of course, there is tension. But Dhoni leads from the front saying,

> *"We will do it. Let's go and play."*

His team members have also shared that a pre-match meeting is usually a 10-15 minute standing affair, nothing fancy. When asked about this, Dhoni said,

> *"Each and every player knows what to do. They are responsible enough. I don't like to tell them (sic)."*

We have to admit that this strategy has worked for the team, because since then, India has seen innumerable victories, world records, and a winning mind-set in all the players.

That Gut Feeling

A winning attitude coupled with a calm mind results in yet another skill – intuition.

Going by a layman's definition of intuition, it is: The 'right-feeling' or 'gut feeling'; the ability to understand something instinctively, without the need for conscious reasoning.

Our captain is known for his intuitive decisions. Dhoni has often admitted to going on the field with his 'gut feeling'. This feeling has been so overpowering that it has spun off a discussion in itself. Researchers started studying it extensively based on Dhoni and established the importance of it. Dhoni has brought into limelight the simplicity and necessity of it at a time when each and every life decision has to be made based on experts' take.

> "He is extremely intuitive and has always flummoxed rivals with his out of the ordinary field placements based purely on his gut feeling, his use of bowlers or his frequent changes in the batting order, which invariably turns matches in his team's favour. This is because he reads the game very well. His extraordinary calm attitude gives him immense mind space to use his conscious and sub-conscious mind effectively."
>
> —Ravi Shastri

Dhoni has set a precedent of such moments when his intuitions proved to be winning matches for him.

When West Indian all-rounder Kieron Pollard walked in to bat for Mumbai Indians at the 2010 IPL finals, Dhoni was quick to place two fielders at extra cover, which in itself is an off-beat decision. But Dhoni played by his instinct and Pollard fell for it. He hit a high cover drive, made contact with the tip of the bat, and the ball landed safe into the hands of the fielder.

Again driving home the point of his instinctive decision making instances, more than a well thought out strategy was when he brought in an inexperienced Joginder Sharma to bowl the last over against Pakistan in the World T20 finals in 2007. Or more recently in IPL4, when opponents Kolkata Knight Riders (KKR) were cruising to victory chasing a modest Chennai Super Kings (CSK) total of 153 runs, Dhoni overlooked the more experienced Scott Styris and handed the ball to Suresh Raina. Equivalently in another IPL match where CSK was playing KKR and the latter needed only 35 runs from 22 balls with 7 wickets in hand, Dhoni's quick-wittedness in bowling changes got the commentary box ticking and no one could stop praising his captaincy. In both the matches, the bowlers delivered and Dhoni's team won.

But the working behind his intuitive mind is again a calm Dhoni. Former Indian cricketer Sunil Gavaskar had once commented that intuition is the working of a calm mind, and Dhoni has it in him.

Most winners display a **strong sense of intuition** in their field of work. But only with the arrival of someone like Mahendra Singh Dhoni, intuition got into the limelight as a concept. Some call Dhoni's unorthodox decision making on field a risk, but adept that he is, he quickly twists and turns the plot and proves every time how a taking a little risk sometimes become necessary and alters the equation in the field. Having an intuition about intuition, Dhoni had already apprehended that this tactic would work. Even though he plans things out in advance, he mostly follows his instincts on field.

While a person cannot always describe, on the logical front, why he had 'a gut feeling' about something, or on what was that feeling based, they are found to be usually correct.

Dhoni's performances reveal that a passion, when closely followed, gives rise to the power of intuition. One can just feel a right judgement without consulting the conscious mind.

Things that don't get registered in our conscious mind don't get lost and find place in the in the sub-conscious. Likewise, intuition is firmly nestled in the sub-conscious.

Our eyes are connected to the brain. So whatever crosses the eyes goes directly to the brain and stays there in the sub-conscious. In time, especially in the time of crisis, people are known to extract information from their sub-conscious without the interference of the conscious mind.

To be aware of the presence of this trait, people can train themselves to be calm and hence become intuitive by nature.

On the road to victory, honing these **intuitive skills** is as important as any other skills and Dhoni plays by it.

These skills, though invisible, create a visible difference in a person's life. They define a winner and a winner's mind. While we work hard and allocate a lot of time and energy into achieving something, putting an effort to acquire these mental skills can be a differentiating factor between mediocrity and a winner. It is easy to ignore them because they sound so simple, but it's very difficult to be simple. Discover your passion and work for it. Be positive. Put in the hard work. Be fearless and keep calm.

Use it. It will help you create the best version of yourself, making you sharper, more efficient and eventually giving you a sense of achievement. Most importantly, it will make you happy.

While the remaining four traits will unveil more secrets about a winner's mind, attitude emerges the strongest trait, because as a stepping stone to anything in life, when you have mastered attitude, working on the remaining becomes easy.

Following chapter is about the importance of setting goals and we will try to decipher the importance of goals as an example set by Dhoni. We will try to understand his goal-setting strategies (which are deadline driven) and how that becomes a priority for him match after match and generally in his life. We will learn how to set goals the Dhoni way, because after concentrating on the right attitude, setting goals the right way can be the game changer.

TWO

Goals

W hat is a goal?

How to read GOALS?

While everyone knows what a goal is, this chapter shows the method of laying it out step-by-step so that you not only have a dream goal for your life; you are also successful in making it come true. Follow the pointers because these are the crucial highlights of Dhoni's success. I have elaborated certain methods. Try to follow them in that order.

> "A goal is a dream with a deadline."
>
> —Napolean Hill

It is said that to achieve anything substantial, you need to put a timeline to it and make it your goal. All abstract dreams and wishes floating in your mind take a definitive shape once you put a deadline to it, like even though Dhoni played a variety of games, once he zeroed down on cricket, he reached his peak. But examples galore of people who don't believe in goals and defer to an 'another time' or a 'someday', and don't appreciate the concept of a deadline. If you try to draw a graph of the lives of these 'someday' people, it would come as a straight, flat line. There are no peaks in their lives.

And then there are people who want to be successful. They have a passion for life, a desire to explore, to dream and to fulfil them, to go beyond and make a difference before they hit the grave. These people, no matter where they come from, seem to move around with an invisible ladder. They need to climb.

'Goal' defines such people.

Winning the World Cup was a double dream for Dhoni. It was the dream of a nation, of its millions for whom cricket is a religion, so Dhoni was burdened with realizing their dreams and fulfilling his. But this dream comes with a deadline which transpires into a GOAL.

Dhoni plays an array of sports. He plays football, basketball, hockey, table tennis and lawn tennis. He is an

"The trouble with not having a goal is that you can spend your life running up and down the field and never reach anywhere."

—BILL COPELAND

accomplished sharpshooter and his stints with bikes are well known. He lounges with his PlayStation and climbs mountains for fun and fitness. He is a complete outdoor person. While most of his childhood he dwindled with all these, the moment he discovered that cricket was his calling, he chaffed through all his hobbies and zeroed down on it. He focussed and worked towards it diligently. Bit by bit, he made his goals, and one by one achieved them when he played various cricketing tournaments at school level.

One goal and one goalpost at a time is what he did that made him the Dhoni we get to see today. It goes beyond saying that he is extremely talented, but setting a goal gave his life a purpose, a direction, and a meaning. It elevated the quality of his life to unimaginable heights.

He made his passion into his goal and achieved success.

> *"If you don't have your own goal in your life, you will be spending the rest of your life fulfilling others'."*

I am a great believer of this thought. Because I have discovered that around the people who pursue a goal are people who don't. These goalless people are unhappily satisfied with running errands for the famous person and to bask in borrowed glories – like a photograph with the hero. They too make their money and live well. But they are never achievers.

Goals are for those people who want to make it count. So tag along and we will see how Dhoni does it.

His Plan

Speaking of how Dhoni achieves his goal, the first thing I will need to write about it is that he does so without much fuss or fanfare. He rather uses some simple guidelines:

1. **Set small goals.**
2. **Simplify your goals.**
3. **Visualization**
4. **Grab and create Opportunity**

While we plan and strategize our goals, it is imperative to keep all these pointers in mind if we want to be a winner.

The goal to the goalpost formula is valid only when we underline the whole thing against a **timeline.**

While we will be discussing in details the uniqueness of Dhoni's goal-setting style, please do not be conned by looking at the simple layout of the goal-to-the-goalpost plan. All the attitude skills that we spoke about in the previous chapter will be required in every layer of the layout.

Unfortunately Dhoni does not have an elixir to hand over, that will allow you to achieve your goal without lifting your finger or working your muscle. That layout above allows you to align you to your goal. It doesn't spell a shortcut. It doesn't rule out hard work. It just makes you more effective. And if this layout is good for Dhoni, it should be good enough for all of us.

So what kind of a goal should we set? Or what kind of goals Dhoni says he sets for himself?

Goals should be achievable yet challenging. While it is said that it should not be so far-fetched that we cannot even visualize it, it should be stretched enough to be titillating.

Experts say that too simple and easy a goal makes it boring, but on the other hand, too stiff ones scare one off.

Therefore, while Australia or Sri Lanka can set a goal for becoming the number one cricket team in the world, it would be too stiff a goal for teams like UAE simply because the other two teams are well-off in cricket.

In the World Cup of 2011, before the Bangladesh team came for the series, their coach gave them an interesting target – to try and bat for all the 50 overs. That, for them, at that point in time, was definitely challenging and worth a chase and now they are one of the competitive sides.

Dhoni likes to set short-term goals that are believable and achievable.

I found it particularly difficult to write this chapter because this is one area he cannot elaborate on. I had to do a lot of coaxing to get what I wanted. My questions like, "What is the ultimate goal of your life?", "What are your plans after retirement?", "Do you think you will captain the next world cup?" and so on were met with a shrug of a shoulder, a smile, an evasive response and nonchalant expressions. The only thing he clearly told me was that he does not like to think much ahead. But as I kept probing,

I realized that his style of goal-setting was unique. He did have a goal for every aspect of his life but they were all short-term ones.

His goals are simple, believable and achievable. This style of setting small goals keeps him focussed without letting him get ruffled by the variety of his interest. He knows how to handle them turn by turn and keep them in the right place.

In the field too, he takes one step at a time. He does not think about the series as a whole or of winning or losing, but plans methodically taking small steps towards achieving his big goal.

So read on. For, this is what I found out and this is what I wrote about what's so special about the concept of setting goals.

1. Set small goals

Dhoni swears by it. Ask him his plans for the fifth match of the series and he will tell you that he doesn't know yet. Ask him the reason and pat comes the reply,

> *"Because I do not believe in thinking so much ahead."*

In the ICC World Cup of 2015 after we lost to Australia in the semis, the media asked Dhoni whether he wished to play the next World Cup. Dhoni laughed and said that it would be a good thing for the media to discuss and analyze.

In the meantime, he had this upcoming IPL League 2015 to focus on.

The strategy that brought home the World Cup 2011:

The strategy, though complicated in the surface, was simple. He lived in the moment, picking up one match at a time. The idea was to go about each match with full concentration without thinking of the remaining matches.

After the team won the World Cup, Virat Kohli was asked how they prepared themselves for the series and what strategy they followed from the beginning to achieve success.

The reply was interpretable. Speaking in consonance with his captain, Kohli, the present vice-captain of the team, accounted that the team just get on beam with the match in hand and not take the extra pressure of winning the cup each time they went to the field. Dhoni's strategy was to not think about the result much and think about the current game. "It was the captain's take. We were supposed to take one match, prepare for it, give it our best and then leave it behind before picking up the next match of the series, till we were on the series. We were not supposed to talk about winning or losing at all. We were only supposed to talk about performing to the best of our ability. I think that strategy worked," Kohli elaborated.

It may sound rather strange to commoners like us who would question if at all **this detachment from the desired result is so important.** The answer to this vital question or rather doubt will be explained in Chapter 3.

Pondering on winning a match, constantly convincing one's mind to win the World Cup, or worrying about the series don't necessarily make one win. Instead, it takes the focus away from the match at hand. Careful strategies and dividing the goal into brief, attainable ones and working on it to the best of our ability makes us win.

When I discussed the cool startegies of our captain, Sourav Ganguly nodded his head in agreement. *Dada* beautifully articulated that performance takes a turn for the worst if one is constantly thinking of hitting a century. "You just have to think of facing the next ball, that's it! No other thought should occupy your mental space," said Ganguly.

"Dhoni never aspired of becoming another Tendulkar," says Wasim, Dhoni's childhood friend. This alone is a living commentary on the temperament of a man who paved his way to greatness; one that is unique; followed but not imitated. "Sachin is God to him even today. He followed him closely. He tried to learn from all the big players, be it Indian or International. But he never compared himself with them. When he started playing Ranji, a couple of us started telling him that he can be as good as them, but he always said that all that was far away. Right now he was enjoying whatever he was doing," Wasim added.

Like a master who has control over his own thought process, Dhoni saw success in setting small goals at a time. His dedication and focus on that small goal produced results which automatically pushed him to the next level, thereby creating his next goal.

Tendulkar was his inspiration, but never his benchmark. He instead focussed on his game with conviction and that brought him to Sachin even to the point of captaining him.

Prior to the Bangladesh-India face-off in World Cup 2015, Dhoni was asked which team – Australia or New Zealand – was his choice of opponents for the semis? Quite stoically Dhoni had put forth that there was still time to it and for the time being his full concentration is on the upcoming match with Bangladesh.

Captaining one of the best cricketing teams of the world, Dhoni naturally has too many things on his mind. But he side-tracks, or more importantly attaches less significance to anything else other than the match at hand. That's exactly why he has a tendency to duck questions on hypothetical situations. He does not like ten different things crowding his mind.

I wanted to study this theory of his in detail, because we all grew up learning that we need to plan and plan for our entire lives.

But Dhoni says that the match at hand has the maximum clarity than something that comes ten days later.

"In this situation now, I know exactly what the challenges are and subsequently what resources are available to me and I am more equipped to deal with it now. People ask me my plans five or ten years down the line, honestly I do have plans but I choose not to over think on them in a way that will hamper my present or stop me from enjoying this moment," Dhoni said.

2. Simplify your goals

"I like to make things simpler for my mind. I like to create simple plans. Once the plans are simple and achievable for the mind, they are easy to execute."

— MSD

A very important exercise if we are trying to achieve something. A goal can be as big as a mountain or the size of a pebble that fits into your fist. It's all a matter of perspective. But in order to convince the mind that a goal can be achieved, it needs to be of an achievable size. It needs to be cut down into bits and pieces and simplified.

We will take an example and show you how Dhoni simplifies a chase.

For example, his team has to chase 200 runs in a 20-20 game from 120 balls.

I wanted to know from Dhoni how he strategizes such matches. I asked him that since he always talks about breaking down big targets into smaller ones, how he did it for this particular match.

"My first attempt is to make a simple plan. 200 in 20 overs is a big total. So I calculate balls to runs. On an average, I

> *assumed that our team can hit 20 fours*
> *in a match. It means 80 runs from 20*
> *balls. 120 runs from 100 balls remained.*
> *That sounds more easy and achievable.*
> *I can see it. So I can achieve it."*

You must be still wondering how this strategy will work for you. On your journey to achieving your main target it will be a string of these very well-planned small goals that will carry you to your destination. If you fail to see or categorize these small goals towards your big one, in all likeliness you will never achieve your big goal.

While a novice sets big, expanded goals with the moon as the destination point, achievers sets small, achievable goals towards that very destination point. The difference is that, a novice usually misses to reach his destination while an achiever, more often than not hits the goalpost!

We sometimes tend to make our dreams look so larger than life, we find it impossible to achieve and hence we have the tendency to give up or worse still, not pursue it at all.

Had Dhoni done the same thing and straight away compared himself to the likes of Sachin Tendulkar and Sourav Ganguly, who are the legends of cricket, he would have had to give up on his dream way back. Instead, he simplified his goals and proceeded step by step till one fine day, he captained Sachin Tendulkar.

This is where the relevance of his thought process

sets in and this **simplification of goal is nothing but an exercise of the mind.** A target of 200 runs will remain the same but skilfully breaking it down to an achievable size will, however, make achieving it easier.

> "World Cup is a year away. Right now I am thinking about the match at hand. That's tomorrow."
> — M.S. Dʜᴏɴɪ during an interview in 2014

With winning always on his mind, Dhoni never lets that same feeling rule his performance. Thinking less of victory or failure, Dhoni **takes one tournament at a time** and plays his game to the best of his ability. More often than not this has always resulted in victory, because his team have been advised by their captain to stay focussed on nothing but the day's game.

Like Dhoni said,

> *"One over at a time. It all adds up in the end."*

Goals are bound to differ from person to person, and so our treatment of goals largely depends on the nature of the goals. They come with shorter or longer life spans and hence the categorization into big lifetime goals and short term goals assume importance.

Like the World Cup can be a long-term goal for Dhoni which will have a five years' timeline, playing soccer tournaments in between for the club and such, will be his short-time goal.

Why is simplifying a goal so important?

The path towards the achievement of your goal is not laden with roses. Like everything in life, this too requires hard work, demanding new skills to be learnt and changes to be affected. Rules in a game keep changing with time and condition. Like Dhoni once said,

> *"The era of playing aggressive cricket and to have the mid-on up is gone. You now try to read the mind-set of a batsman."*

The recognition of the presence of mind game has changed the face of cricket for good. Only a person with a clear vision of that goal can after clearly visualizing the hurdles towards his goal, simplify it, strategize and deal with such developments.

Dhoni's off-beat field strategy that has brought home the trophy quite a number of times is now a hot button in the world. His field layout is not just a cricketing marvel but it takes into account each and every opponent and their individual strengths and weaknesses.

His mantra is always **keep it simple**. Having advocated time and again cricket to be a very simple game, Dhoni's approach towards the game has always been uncluttered and soluble. Always experimenting with new techniques, innovations such as randomly switching bowlers, Dhoni believes, that if *this* strategy does not work, then *that* will. His accurate analysis of the match and his immense ability to take on the spot decisions, which has been a subject of study in many B-schools across the world, is attributed to this quality of keeping things simple.

Too many 'what ifs' or 'then whats' paralyze the thought process. Simplifying the goal allows you to come up with soluble ideas even if they are considered unorthodox and helps you remain flexible in order to strategically achieve your goal.

> *"I keep it simple. I do not like to crowd my mind with too many thoughts. That gives me space in my mind to strategize it as per requirement."*

These were his exact words when asked what was going through his mind when he gave the ball first to Ravindra Jadeja instead of R. Ashwin in World Cup 2015 against South Africa, which is the normal protocol.

Well, we won that match.

So, let's see how keeping things simple in his mind made him more effective.

South Africa had a good line-up of left-handed batsmen and Dhoni utilized this situation. He strategically brought in left-arm Jadeja to bowl to SA's right-handed opener. When the sides changed to a left-handed batsman, Dhoni gave the ball Ashwin, who is a right-arm bowler. Dhoni changed the order taking into account the opposition's characteristics.

A simple strategy, often tried and tested in cricket, Dhoni didn't waste time thinking over it but rather made quick changes in the bowling order. His mind was not possessed with the effects of his decisions backfiring; neither did he budge thinking what if the strategy resulted in India losing the game.

Things to be aware of while setting a goal and dividing it up

First, we have to make up our mind and the goal should be acceptable to the mind. It's not difficult to achieve that clarity of mind if we waste less time on over thinking and complicating it by conjuring up unnecessary hypothetical situations.

Often we have seen great plans failing because of wrong execution. That is why goals need to be approached with a **soluble-doable** method. It has to be such that it can be worked upon.

It is also important for goals to be flexible because it's not necessary that the approach towards it will always be the same tried and tested one. There are various ways of reaching a goal, precisely why we have back-ups. So, if Plan A fails we have a Plan B to fall back on. Make your goals flexible and it will make it easier for you to achieve it.

"When on the field we cannot predict every action of the opponent. Things happen outside the plan. So taking an on-the-spot decision becomes easier if the team adapts quickly to a new plan when the original one does not seem to be working too well."

—MS DHONI

This only holds good when the target is not blurred. That allows you to make instinctive decisions and find alternative ways of achieving that target. And this holds true for aspect of life, let alone cricket.

3. Visualization

Even before I start talking about visualization, I would ask my readers not to get confused between the concept of visualization and thinking about the end result.

While thinking about the end result, overthinking and obsessing about it is a negative trait of the mind, whereas visualization is a technique. It is much like setting on a journey from point A to point B where, when you set off from point A you can clearly see your destination point B and drive towards it.

After winning World Cup 2011, Dhoni had said that he could clearly visualize himself holding the cup even before the series started. This is visualization, which is a very important exercise in the path of setting a goal.

How does it work?

You set a goal

↓

You fix a goalpost

↓

You visualize yourself getting the desired
result to your goalpost

↓

You start off on your journey.

Why is visualization a technique?

If we want to win, we need to sit calm for a few minutes
and visualize a win. Once it is done, we need to leave it
at that and concentrate on the journey and not think about
the destination.

Visualization allows our neurological senses to align
ourselves to our desired results. This technique is a one-
time power-play of the mind and not a constant run leading
to obsession.

4. Opportunities

Please consider these questions:

- *What if you are good at acting or dancing but no
  one gives you an opportunity to showcase them?*

- *What if you have all the relevant degrees but you don't get the job of your dreams?*

Or

- *What if you are confident that you can score more but no one gives you the opportunity?*

When you feel that no one is giving you the opportunity you deserve, do it the Dhoni way – create one.

> "Sometimes opportunities will not knock. You will have to create them"
>
> —MS DHONI

Of course opportunities were not laid out in a plate for Dhoni. While he was fortunate with some 'given' opportunities, the others vanished in no time, even before presenting themselves. For Dhoni, who mostly played football, cricket was something he chanced upon. It was his school coach Keshav Ranjan Banerjee who advised Dhoni to fill in the wicket-keeper's position in the school team after the former wicket-keeper got promoted to tenth grade and as per rules the tenth graders were not allowed to be in the team for their school finals. And Dhoni chipped in.

But again it was not always easy for Dhoni. While one opportunity was given the others he created for himself. During an inter-school match Dhoni insisted his coach promote him to number 1 from number 7. An unsure Banerjee refused a number of times, but relented later as Dhoni never stopped pursuing. But that nod was not without reservations. Throwing a challenge at Dhoni, Banerjee had said he would not keep the next batsman padded, as when he was taking a risk with Dhoni, he would want him to finish the match. An undeterred Dhoni went on to score 213 runs, putting up a partnership of 400+ runs with Shabbir Ahmed which proudly finds mention in the Limca Book of Records.

That was Dhoni's best knock in the initial days. He wowed the crowd who were simply enthralled witnessing the skyrocketing heights the ball went to. That match became a talking point everywhere bringing immense laurels to Dhoni.

Another similar incident could go down in history as an example in persuasiveness and confirm Dhoni to be the man who never knew what it is to give up. Chanchal Bhattacharya, the first formal coach of Dhoni in Jharkhand, had initially refused to take him under his tutelage. Bhattacharya said,

> *"There were lots of boys already in the batch and I did not see anything extraordinary in this boy to go out of my way and give him a place."*

But Dhoni never stopped persuading him. Dhoni would always be around his academy requesting him for a five-minute opportunity with the ball.

"I would see him just sitting in the periphery of the ground. He used to keep looking at me and waiting for me to call him. Sometimes I was too busy. And sometimes I would call him, hand over the ball to him and say, 'Just five minutes, ok?' He would smile and be very happy,"

recounted Bhattacharya. And that turned out to be the deciding minutes in Dhoni's life, because every time it would stretch to **15, 20 or even 30 minutes, when he bowled, batted or just dribbled making Bhattacharya notice his passion.**

"I knew that if this boy did not have talent, he will acquire it. His passion will drive him to excellence," said Bhattacharya.

The decision had already been made and Dhoni got his first formal coach in Bhattacharya. Today in any talk show when Bhattacharya is asked to comment on his student and the captain of Team India, his voice gives away nothing but pride for that young boy who once waited for hours just to spend *five* minutes with the ball. Dhoni created an opportunity after opportune moments refused to happen to him and he made cricket happen to him.

For most of us who believe in sitting and crying for things to happen and complaining about the lack of opportunities, the awareness of this concept is the answer.

When passion drives you, opportunity can never be an issue – either you have them or you create them.

It's important to **recognize the concept of opportunities** and be in the **receiving mode.** Receiving mode means you are in a position to grab or create an opportunity when such a situation arrives. Most importantly when you want to carve out a niche and become 'something' you need to place yourself in the receiving mode. For example – if you want to be an actor, you need to learn acting, so that when an opportunity for acting arrives, you are well equipped and ready to 'receive'. If you want to be a sports person, you need to play, eat well, keep fit, and learn your sport in order to be in the receiving mode. And the list goes on for every career opportunity that may come your way. Once you are in the receiving mode you are already in the process and while in that you can create an opportunity or grab one. To be in the process you have to follow the process.

Coming back to explaining with taking the captain as our reference, Dhoni wanted to be a cricketer, so it was important for him to play cricket, even if it meant playing gully cricket. But he didn't leave it at that.

Being in the process does not just mean doing what you are doing. It involves a little more than that. It envelops learning, looking for opportunities, and having the right attitude. When Bhattacharya refused to coach Dhoni, his ego and confidence, both could have taken a beating. But he kept his hopes high and persuaded the coach till he got what he wanted.

A person in the receiving mode confronts opportunities more often than a person who is mostly pessimistic.

What is an opportunity?

Skipping what the lexicon would have to offer, opportunity is a chance that allows you to reach your final goal or a series of big and small chances that sets you on the path of that same goal. It does not mean lack of adversity. It means that even in an adverse situation, a winner knows how to overcome it and grab/create an opportunity.

In a press interview Dhoni said that he learnt most of his cricket by playing in the narrow alleys of Ranchi with his friends.

That, for him, was opportunity. Faced with adversities, Dhoni didn't sit back twiddling his thumb waiting for Team India to make him one of Men in Blue. He opened himself up to new experiences, took his chances, and set the wheel rolling by being in the process and treated each one of them as an opportunity. He didn't underestimate opportunities and didn't let go off even a miniscule of them. He took away something from each experience and made himself available for many. Never wasting time off the field, he carried on playing. He played cricket with canvas balls. He played for his school team. He played for clubs. When it rained, he played football. Each one of these experiences was opportunities that had built him up to the final slot – Team India.

No experience is too big or small. If one waits for the final big thing to happen, it usually never happens because the process was skipped. While it's important to enhance your skills, it's also important to look out for such experiences, take chances and treat it as an opportunity. And the most important trick is to recognize an opportunity as an opportunity.

Taking those chances makes you aware of your strengths and weaknesses. It gives you the opportunity to learn more towards your area of interest. And it takes you closer to your goal.

Identify Your Unique Selling Point

Dhoni is a hard hitter of the ball. That was one of the things that brought him to the limelight when he was asked to go in at number 3 as a pinch-hitter against a match with Pakistan. Being a hard-hitter is his Unique Selling Point (USP).

Let's count what else he has as his USP:

1. **His fearlessness makes him stand apart**
2. **His calmness is a talking point**
3. **His leadership style is a 'to-learn' topic**
4. **His unorthodox decision-making ability is highly acknowledged**

These made him stand tall and apart. While every cricketer has his own USP, it becomes very important to identify the same and prove your uniqueness to the world. Discovering them will make you a winner.

No one has ever become great by trying to be like someone else. A 'like someone' has so place in the world. They are the most neglected bunch in the universe, no matter how close you are to your 'hero'. The moment you pin your goalpost to be 'like' that person, you have already lost your battle.

So readers, what's your USP?

The power of choice

This may sound a little off the track, but I have to talk about it because I have seen Dhoni practicing it diligently and have come to acknowledge the importance of it in the path to success, happiness, and winning. I have realized that if you do not have the power to choose, you can never win. Most of all, you will never be happy. This is the one thing you will need to possess first, before possessing anything else. And when in the process of setting your goal, never let go of it for a single second.

> "The only reason we don't have what we want in life is the reasons we create why we can't have them."
>
> —TONY ROBBINS

So, what is this power of choice?

Coming from a humble background, he didn't opt for a run-of-the-mill secured job to earn his bread and butter; he chose to pursue his hobby instead. And if there is one person on earth who has the power of choice, it's none other than Dhoni. When he wins, he chooses not to get carried away by it. When he loses, he chooses not to become a failure. This World Cup semi-final 2015, after his team lost to Australia, Dhoni said that,

> *"Only one team can win a match. This time it was their turn."*

He added that they have done well in the series and the bowlers have learnt a lot. He chose to see a loss as a learning experience other than treating it as a defeat. He plays cricket because he chooses to do so and not because someone lets him do it. The day he decides he is done with cricket will be the day he will quit cricket the way he quit the Test format.

When I broached the topic of Dhoni quitting the Test format, veteran sports journalist Debashish Dutta said, "Look Sfurti, there is no spicy story for me to tell you here. The media is cooking up a lot, but Dhoni had been talking about quitting any of the one formats (either T20, Test, ODI's), especially the Test format, for two-three years now. He said it was too much for him. He also says that when he plays, he plays in his own terms. He does not want any grand farewell; his farewell will be for himself, quiet. He told me once that he will not give anyone the chance to kick him out. Rather, the day he felt he was done, he would leave on his own. He does not play for anybody. He plays for himself."

Dhoni has taught me never to be in a situation in which I would be at the mercy of anybody or anything, or for that matter, any situation, condition, hurdles, fear, greed, or ignorance. The knowledge of the power of choice is immensely powerful if only one realizes the absolute necessity of it in the path to becoming a winner.

Drawing an end to this chapter, it's my request to my readers that you should choose your goal; you should never mind if you win or lose, and not forget to tally. To tally means to sit back and see what you have done right, what you have done wrong, and identify areas you need to work upon. Tallying scores help to chisel your skills as you proceed towards your final goal. It makes one learn.

And what did I learn?

Well, almost everything. Some I did count upon, others I did not.

As I sat down to pen this book on the great phenomenon called Dhoni, I did not take into account that my life would change, or the fact that he would teach me things which I thought I already knew, but didn't really.

And I realized while I thought about the broader aspects

of life, I forgot simple things like being positive or staying focussed. This book and one on whom this is written about taught me the importance of setting small, sharp goals. These are again very simple things that we all know. But Dhoni has taken all these to a whole new level where they weigh heavy. And possessing these simple traits with conviction makes you so powerful that you move around with an aura about you.

Dhoni has it and when I met him, I felt it too. It was enlightening to find an aura in a simple person with simple beliefs. He made me believe that I can achieve anything I want to with hard work and faith. He taught me to keep things simple, to be fearless, and dare to live my dream. Above all, he has made me a good human being. The heady mix of his power packed celebrity aura and simplicity of his self was intoxicating. That itself is something to learn and the very knowledge of it will bring everything else in your life.

He also taught me the power of honesty, the power of being true to yourself, and the power of being a good person. I knew being good was great, but didn't know that being good was powerful too.

And it felt cool!

The Bottom-Line:

- **Set small goals, may be weekly. It keeps you focussed, enhances your productivity.**

- Your goal should be simple and easy for your mind. Whatever is inside is outside; simpler inside, simpler outside!

- If opportunity doesn't knock, create one!

- It's not how talented you are; it's how courageous you are!

- Stop Overthinking! Keep it simple.

THREE

Follow the Process

> "I believe in giving more than 100% on the field and I don't really worry about the results. If there's great commitment on the field, that's victory for me."
>
> —MS Dhoni

I have forever been enchanted with this theory of his. We have heard Dhoni many a time, so when I finally got the opportunity to meet him, I could not resist asking him to give a talk on this whole concept. What is this whole idea about *not worrying about the final outcome?* I asked Dhoni, if this attitude makes him a winner. I asked him to tell me about a few Dhoni-principles that I can pin down as a takeaway for my readers. I had so many questions that it made him laugh. He said,

"I always follow the process."

'Follow the process' is his pet phrase. Though we have often heard him say that, the very idea was vague to me until he explained it to me. I asked him, "What do you actually mean by it? Let's say that I have a job interview tomorrow and I am mighty nervous about it. How do you suggest I prepare myself? In this given scenario, how do you apply this 'follow the process' concept?"

He looked at me straight and said, "Is fear a part of process?"

I said, "NO".

"What is part of the process? Preparation. Then you need to do just that!"

He sat me down and went on explaining, "Fear, negative thoughts and all other self-limiting thoughts are the things that come before a big day. To follow the process would be to focus on preparation. Eliminate everything that's not required for the interview tomorrow. Like anxiety about the interview, nervousness, overthinking, or losing sleep at night. All these are not in the process. What's in the process is knowing your subject, acquiring relevant skill set, resting well so that you are fresh and your mind is aware. Think about how to dress up appropriately and reaching the venue on time. And once you are there, give your 100%. That's all. That's the correct procedure. **There are no other procedures other than that to follow the process.**"

If you are afraid, just ask yourself: "Is fear a part of Process?"

We affix a goal and strengthen it with the right attitude. But if we cannot follow the process, winning will always elude us. What he said was simple. We complicate things by overthinking.

We have seen great players acting funny on the verge of defeat. So even if there is a 10% chance of turning the game into their favour, they can't. The only reason being they have failed to follow the process. Fear grips their nerves, doubt shrouds them, faith hits the rock bottom, and hope leaves them. Maybe a well calculated 6 and a 2 would have brought home the cup, but how many can? Those who consistently can is because they can follow the process, while those who more often can't, do not know the art.

Like Sourav Ganguly said, "There are no tough days or soft days for me. I just keep going."

Dhoni says that in order to reach from point A to B, there is always a process that needs to be followed. And everything that's not in the process needs to be eliminated. This practice helps maintain focus, helps keep the deadline, creates opportunity for higher level of consistency, thereby making the '100%' happen. Like, he says, when he and his team go out to play a match, what lies in the process is planning and strategizing to win, motivating the team, laying down a game plan,

What lies in the process?

Positive Thoughts, Preparation, Calmness, Clarity

and then finally playing it out there. On the contrary, what does not lie in the process and hence needs to be eliminated is worrying about the result, fearing the opposition, getting demotivated because of previous defeats, being overconfident because of previous victories, thinking about media reaction/ public outrage/ social media uproar in the face of a possible defeat and all things along those lines.

What doesn't lie in the process? Fear, Confusion, Overthinking

This is Dhoni's mantra for every aspect of his life, "Follow the Process. Get into the flow. Leave everything behind and give the job your 100%." For him, a World Cup final has no more or no less importance than a seasonal tri-series. This helps keep his nerves in a tight leash and helps him do whatever is required to do to win a match. Recalling an example from Chapter 2 where Dhoni said he slept well before his debut match as he had to remain fresh in the morning, it was part of following the process. His fellow players too mentioned that while once in a while they lose sleep, especially before a match with Pakistan or Australia, they have never seen Dhoni do so. They said that Dhoni sleeps tight and advises everyone to do the same.

In Chapter 1 we spoke of hard work and there we mentioned that we will discuss Dhoni's method of hard work in this chapter.

Arriving at the answer, I gathered that Dhoni's way of hard work is not to simply slog like a donkey. He follows the process while he puts in the labour.

He prepares himself mentally too and thus he is someone who is known for his absolute clarity of mind. He keeps his days sorted, never getting confused or unnecessary blocking the mind. He doesn't answer phone calls and never reads newspapers, especially the sports section.

Why?

Dhoni just doesn't work hard, he tunes in a fair bit of smartness into it. Starting his career as a wicket-keeper, he gradually climbed up the ladder and became an accomplished batsman. He recognized his strength as a hard-hitter and made those amazing records. He recognized his weaknesses and honed his skills. He used his mental skills to learn the game so well that he became the captain in fast track. Not only did he play the game well, he learned to motivate his teammates and understood the importance of building a strong team spirit. At times of crisis, when he and his team performed poorly, he knew how to get out of that demotivating situation and bring the team to its peak performance.

He knows the value of positive attitude as a way to winning. He handles media effectively and at the same time doesn't get pressurized by outside forces, fans, and criticism. This is not just playing well or working hard, this is smart work. It is a 360 degree approach to the game. It's how he followed the process completely – end to end.

Along with the basic skill sets that a person is born with or acquire in the line of their passion, developing these 360 degree approach becomes vital too.

Every game has a laid down process. Be it studying, playing, running a corporate house, or running a household, it has a set process. To be successful in anything you do, the process cannot be denied. Every successful man has consciously or sub-consciously followed it.

Dhoni says:

- **Keep your negative emotions aside and do what you are actually supposed to do**
- **Eliminate fear**
- **Evaluate your mind and separate out mental resistance**
- **Keep things simple**
- **Every job has steps to be followed that are relevant to the job. Follow those steps and eliminate everything that's unnecessary.**

For instance, when his daughter Ziva was born, Dhoni was in Australia with less than two weeks left for the World Cup 2015 to commence. One of our sources shared that Dhoni was an extremely happy man when he announced the birth of his daughter. He constantly kept in touch with his wife Sakshi and relatives back home to check on the welfare of his new born and his wife. The name 'Ziva' was his idea. He was very much involved in the naming ceremony of his daughter and made frequent phone calls. But he didn't consider making a trip home. When others suggested he made a quick trip to see his daughter, Dhoni pointed it out that it was a long way back home. Too many stopovers and changing flights would make it a close cut and he just wanted to concentrate on the upcoming series. World Cup was important. He did not want any distractions. Later he said he was on a national duty so everything else could wait.

To give you a more vivid outline on how to 'Follow the Process', I give an example to make you understand the process well. If you aspire to be a cricketer and want to make it to the national team, the steps to be followed are – play a lot of cricket, grab every opportunity without judging whether the opportunity is big or small, follow a strict dietary regime, believe in yourself, and never lose hope.

Following the process would mean scheduling each of these steps and following them relentlessly. Anything that comes in between are excuses and mental blocks. They need to be identified and methodically eliminated as they will hinder the process of achieving the goal. When Dhoni advices to follow the process, he is always referring to it in terms of the job at hand which for him is usually the next match. He consciously never thinks too much of the future, neither is he a huge believer of planning much ahead.

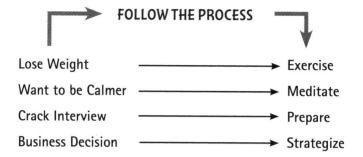

But as I breakdown the winner's mind of Dhoni, we can well decipher that all these qualities are not necessarily those that a person possesses only by birth. They can be acquired by understanding them and practicing them. All winners are not winners by birth. They have also lost now and then. In fact most of them have started their life with losing. Their stories of losses have been written large on the walls of success alongside their stories of winning.

Why?

We have all grown up reading 'failure is the pillar to success' and we shouldn't take it lightly. When we see the failures of great achievers being eulogized, it is done with a purpose. It teaches us to grab our chance so that we too can find our own way as they did. Looking at their defeats and victories, we should be able to ask ourselves the million dollar question: "If they can, why can't I?"

No one becomes a champion overnight. It happens only in films. In life, to become a champion, the process should be followed – end to end. Like a person who weighs 100kgs and is trying to lose weight, going to the gym is not enough. To follow the complete process, he has to get himself into a strict dietary regime and has to maintain that daily. First and foremost, he **has to believe in himself and not lose hope and he should rule out negative thoughts.** That is the entire process and if he can't do it in its entirety, success will always elude him.

It's paramount to keep in mind that the process does not come with a guarantee card. **It includes losing, getting frustrated, falling, losing hope and sometimes thoughts of quitting.** But a strong scaffolding of mental skills will make us overcome all these negative thoughts and get saddled on the horse's back. A journey from a speck of dust to stardom is not as we see in the movies. Interestingly, it's much more!

To make life count, to make a difference and stand out, to make dreams come true, a lot of hard work is involved. Try every trick you know, but never try to replace this 'follow the process' concept with any brilliant idea pulled out from your sleeves.

It doesn't work.

It takes not just talent but a strong base of mental skills to become a winner.

And being aware of the existence of such skills is the first step towards achieving them. Some people like Dhoni are born with it, while others acquire it. **My quest to unravel these very mental skills of Dhoni was to prove to the world that they are achievable.** In this entire book,

I have picked up his statements and broke them down to their base meanings for my readers – like 'follow the process' is a matter of attitude, because Dhoni never uses the word 'attitude'. But when he says follow the process, he displays great attitude, his ability to give 100% and to remain aloof from the outcome.

I believe that everyone knows the concept today in some form or the other, but Dhoni not only knows it in its totality, he is one of those few people who has executed it in reality and that's why he is a champion.

What did he achieve through this? The supreme power to give his 100% to the game.

Dhoni has been declared as the **fifth most valuable athlete on the planet** by Forbes magazine in 2014.

That's the work of a champion. His deftness with his bat and ball is a job well accomplished. But Dhoni, in the process, made huge difference to the sport of cricket as well. He redefined aggression on the field with a dignity of decency, which means he is neither rude nor wild or arrogant. His calmness has set up a new benchmark in the field, because losing your temper is not a part of the process. It has the potential to upset your psychological form. So an entire overhauling of the mind game got into roll as a parallel game form in the field. His approach to the game in the field was fresh, something people were forced to stop and speculate, learn, admire, and appreciate. In the last World Cup, the commentators couldn't stop mentioning his calmness every time the camera panned towards him. His stand in the dressing room too was like a paradigm shift. He had a different thought process and handled the media intelligently. There was a 360 degree approach to the game besides the game itself.

> *"It takes practice to learn the art and then more practice to learn it good and then some more to do it in the best of your ability and still more practice to challenge every single achieved self-best. It sometimes takes a lifetime,"*

says Dhoni.

"*Karm kar, phal ki asha maat kar.*" The line from the *Bhagavad Gita*, literally translates into 'Do you job, do not think about the result'.

It's an age-old saying which finds mention in most religious texts. Buddha quoted it and many a great men and women have followed it. Over the centuries, people have verified it, in different languages and expressions. And yet the absolute thrust of it eludes us. Barring a few, men have failed to grasp this concept in its totality – **the power of giving 100%.**

This emanates from a strong mind where you have to first convince your mind to accomplish a job. Men have ridden around the world and conquered heaven and hell, but have failed to conquer their own mind. And this in itself is proof enough of how strong our mind is. Like an unruly beast, it romps around and controls our life. But when leashed and used to our advantage, this very beast can make you win!

Generations before us would swear by this a lot, like my grandmother used to chant it to me from the *Gita*. These universal lines bored me at that tender age because Dhoni hadn't yet happened me then.

But Dhoni has understood it and understood it well. As he told me, "Giving your 100% is all you can do. That's in your hand. The result isn't."

In *Gita* what Krishna said to Arjuna was that once a target is identified, his focus should be on the arrow. If his focus is on the target, he will never be able to shoot the arrow correctly. To interpret that, Arjuna's aim should be on the arrow, which is in his control and not the target, which is far away and therefore out of his reach.

> "I never worried if I was not selected for a tournament and just concentrated on my game,"
> —MS DHONI said in a panel discussion moderated by commentator Harsha Bhogle

This attitude is not easy to come by. A world of expectation is built around the end result without actually putting in that 100% required to achieve the result. Ask around and more often than not you will find people talking about their target and not the effort they are putting in. And when we fail to hit the target, something dies within.

Therefore, to bring your mind to that level where you are putting in that effort yet you are calm about the result is mandatory and at the same time an extremely difficult job. A success story like Dhoni's is not an easy one. It needs a lot of mind-training to attain that point.

Obsessing & Overthinking

This thought about the end result is again associated with overthinking, which silently works its way and takes us far from that result. The way to eliminate this trait in yourself is to first identify it within you. Ask yourself – "Am I by nature an obsessive person? Am I an overthinker?"

Dhoni is a virtuoso because he eliminates overthinking from his game and keeps it simple. The ability to keep things simple and obliterate obsessiveness and overthinking is all that makes the difference between a winner and a loser.

In the second test match of England vs India 2014 (Pataudi Trophy), India won the match by 95 runs. Ishant Sharma earned his career's best figure of 7/74 and was crowned Man of the Match. Ishant Sharma credited his huge success to captain MS Dhoni. He said that the captain had asked him to throw bouncers. Sharma further added that he was sceptical about it in the beginning. But Dhoni insisted saying,

> *"You are tall enough. You should try the bouncers."*

Obsession is an extreme mental state that paralyses the logical thought process and affects our decision making abilities. The fact that Dhoni told Sharma that he should try bouncers was logical thinking of a calm mind that is free of pressure. In the post-match presentation, Sharma said that his excellent performance and all the wickets belong to the captain. "He is the one man who knows how to keep things in perspective and motivate players to get the best out of them. He does not obsess or overthink. He keeps things relaxed," he added.

As a counter example, South Africa, being an excellent team, could never win a World Cup because of obsession. They are known as 'chokers' in the world of cricket because their style of losing can only be described as 'choked with obsession'. Even though they have had one of the best batting line-ups, bowlers, and powerful fielding, they choke during World Cups. Their obsession with the trophy makes them lose focus.

During the last World Cup in the match between South Africa and New Zealand, SA was on the winning side. But somehow they failed miserably in the last 5-7 overs. Their strong and steady fielding messed up and the greatest of them all. AB de Villiers missed a run out, let alone too many extra runs and misfielding that happened in the last few overs. Powerful South Africans missed it by that much and lost the match to New Zealand.

Obsessed with winning, we have witnessed numerous activities on the field that have ultimately resulted in a loss. Batsmen throwing the bat when declared out or the bowler abusing mindlessly after he bagged one wicket are all signs of an over excited mind. But no one has ever seen such heightened reactions from Dhoni on or off field. He is always his calm self and a master at that. His stability is rock solid and all kind of negative emotions are well dealt with from within.

FAF (Fear, Anger, Frustration)

Time and again, Dhoni has been vocal about fighting FAF. Fearless as he is, his face betrays no frustration **and therefore he emerges a winner even if he has lost**.

In an interview, cricketer Amit Mishra had said that while he had been kept out of several matches, Dhoni had advised him never to stop practicing, keeping these three negative traits far from his psychological orbit. Not just Misra, Dhoni has this advice for all his team mates.

Many readers will identify with this. Whenever they were angry or frustrated or operated under fear, they ruined things for themselves.

But how do we follow the process? How do we stop overthinking or keep FAF aside, which are nothing but natural emotions. Dhoni says that in order to beat these emotions we need to inculcate the habit of distancing ourselves a little from the end result, bringing us back to that *shloka* from *Gita: "Karm kar, phal ki asha maat kar."*

And with this, we come to a very powerful section of the book – **Detachment.**

Detachment

How do we work towards a goal without thinking about the result? How to not get frustrated when we fail, or stop fear from creeping in before the big day? How do we control anger when things don't go according to the plan?

The answer is **Detachment.**

Even after losing the Border-Gavaskar Trophy badly against Australia in Australia, the Indian team played for around three months in Australia and hardly won a game. Still they came up fresh for the World Cup. Though they lost to Australia in semis, India managed to win seven consecutive games.

For Dhoni, every match is a fresh start and he approaches each match with a fresh mind completely detaching himself from the before and the after, the to-be and the not-to-be. That detachment allows him to give 100% every time and makes him win.

When we have a goal, distancing ourselves from the end result will help us give in that vital 100% in order to win.

Dhoni's detachment from anything and everything other than the game is something that has come to the notice of cricket experts around the globe. His calm attitude brings in the feeling that nothing really matters to him much.

"The day I decide I am done with cricket, will be the day I will pack my bags and take off."

—MS Dhoni during a press conference after Team India lost to Australia in the ICC Cricket World Cup semi-finals in 2015.

"I believe in the process more than the result. If you are properly prepared, physically and mentally committed to the task, and fully engaged in the moment, then I have no problem with the outcome."

—MS Dhoni

We don't see him jumping with joy when a match is won, neither do we see him sulk in the face of loss. He always wears a smile. Right after the day India lost to Australia in the World Cup semis he was smiling nice and warm. He definitely did not come across as a broken, devastated captain. He didn't even bother to portray that image. He is never apologetic. He looked happy and contended and said that the team played very well throughout the tournament. He also said that in a match, only one team can win and this time it was the turn of the Aussies.

This POV only becomes possible through detachment and for one who can analyse things from a third party perspective without getting personal.

It's difficult to achieve that kind if detachment about something for which you have shed your sweat and blood only a few minutes ago. But only by achieving this POV will you be able to set your mind free from the past and move ahead.

For every setback that Dhoni had faced, he detached himself promptly, plucked the learning point, and moved ahead. One of the reasons why he was made the captain in the shortest of duration leaving aside all the experienced players is because of his ability to move ahead fast. He proved his strength every time because he carries no baggage. And he wasted no time in proving the selectors right by bringing home the T20 World Cup for India in 2007.

To bring home the point of detachment more appropriately, we have to recall here another chapter of his life that has already been dealt with before. But the repetition becomes necessary and how! Because getting to know that a beautiful gift waited him back home when he was way on 'national duty' was not a thing to be taken for granted, and Dhoni didn't. He just did what he thought was necessary at that moment and responded to his call of duty. Two weeks before the ICC Cricket World Cup 2015, his wife Sakshi delivered their daughter Ziva. The news was enough to send the press into a tizzy, but a dedicated Dhoni didn't fly home as much as he would have wanted to. He had pinpoint focus on the upcoming series as he maintained the necessary detachment in order to sustain and win every single match till the semi-finals. Only after the team got knocked out of the tournament did Dhoni go home to his newborn daughter. Later, holding Ziva, an elated father had said that the sight of his little daughter has **changed his life forever.**

To further demonstrate his commitment towards the concept let's take a look at another moment from Dhoni's life.

When Dhoni had started playing the ODIs, he had requested his parents not to come for the matches as their presence distracted him. Now, that is the truest definition of detachment, wherein none other than Dhoni changed the set rules and defining it anew for the world. His success story still continues as I write this and people still call him lucky. But behind all this 'luck' is a strong mind at work that made this success story possible.

> "Luck is not a solo job. It is a combination of hard work, commitment and the right mix of attitude."
>
> —Anonymous

Thinking and overthinking lead to confusion. Since our mind is never at rest, we race forward and think every possible outcome. Then we pull back to the past and bring up similar situations. After that we compare and contrast in all possible permutations and combinations till our mind becomes tired.

I'm sure readers will identify with exactly what I am saying; the crazy rounds, circles, and loops our mind makes of certain events!

"Dhoni never overthinks, this is his most significant strength."
— ZAHEER KHAN, Dhoni's colleague & cricketer.

It has already been proved that the mind is more powerful than the body. So when the body is tired, but the mind is still throbbing with the energy of our passion, we can still go ahead and perform. When the mind is tired, it tends to give up and comes to a point where it does not care about anything. A tired mind defeats the possibility of victory. A detached mind is seldom tired.

In the process of doing a job, while it is permissible for the body to get tired, which can be rejuvenated in no time with a little bit of rest and some good food, rejuvenating a tired and defeated mind is not easy. A defeated mind will see a hurdle as a huge setback and will tend to give up. If we keep ourselves detached from the end result, the mind is still fresh to overcome any hurdle or fight a setback, and that's all that's required to win in life – the ability to sustain and fight back.

ATTACHMENT ➝ THINKING ➝ OVERTHINKING ➝ OBSESSING

While doing research for this book, I used to frequently visit Ranchi. During one of those visits, I spoke to one of Dhoni's childhood friend – with whom he shared field during his school days and still do whenever Dhoni is in town. This player was considered better than Dhoni in terms of technique and his batting abilities. While talking to him, I came across something very meaningful. He said that when he was given a chance to play for the next level,

"I was under a lot of pressure. Thousands of 'what if's' surrounded my mind. The opportunity seemed too large and I perceived myself too small. 'What will people think' killed me. My constant useless imagination led me to an inevitable failure."

"Seriously Sfurti," he said, "this thought has done all the damage and I still regret it. If I would have controlled my destructive thoughts about winning or losing, I could have at least gone out there and played."

When we spoke of Dhoni, he said,

"But Mahi was sorted. He has a still mind. During those days when I spoke to him about my fears, all he kept saying was, 'Keep playing and focus on your game. Everything else will be fine.' But I never understood. I truly believe that every person should know the importance of mental skills at a very early stage."

When a person is obsessed about the result and has little patience in the process, a hurdle or an impediment in the way makes him give it up easily. It means he lacks **consistency**. And a person lacking in consistency tends to quickly lose interest and shifts his focus to something else which is new and feels easier to achieve. And this switching goes on until it becomes his trait.

Worse, if a person is not **aware** of this trait, it becomes his pattern and remains with him throughout his life. You will come across people who will tell you that they tried thousands of jobs or looked through various business options in their life but fate was against them.

> "Failing once is just a condition with a timeline that will come to an end. Giving up is what makes failure permanent."
>
> —Anonymous

Dhoni's mind is alert to kinds of skills. He knows how extremely powerful the mind is and that it can achieve everything it sets its focus on. He knows the importance of hard work, consistency and calmness. He knows the relevance of keeping aside FAF if one wants to be a winner. He knows what it means to follow the process and giving 100 percent. He also knows the concept of detachment. He knows the phrase 'because I can'. He understands all these like no one else and uses them in his path to winning. That's called '**being aware**'.

Being aware means bringing the mind to that 100% state, where we give our mind the opportunity, enough available mind space, and a fertile ground, where every bit of detail gets registered that's in the conscious mind. Increasing the awareness level will enable us to give that 100% despite the various distractions surrounding us.

We all must have solved this puzzle of finding this 10-12 minute differences between two similar pictures – a feather missing here, a cap missing there. We must have also noticed that while some people can spot these differences in a jiffy, others take time to complete it, while others cannot go beyond pointing out 4-5 differences. Although all of them have perfect pairs of functioning eyes and see the same things, awareness level differs. This is the crux of an aware mind – the power of observation. It's the ability to draw from the mind and evaluate it at the time of need.

Consider this:

A U-16 or U-19 cricket player, even though he knows very well the merit of hard work, knows about the power of concentration and its implication in the long run, fails to take action because of his lack of awareness. So when his seniors and coaches chant the same mantra over and again about focus and hard work, he is irritated and utterly bored.

He doesn't understand much of mental skills. At that age, his mind is everywhere. He doesn't know how to control his mind and channel it in the right direction. He has no control over FAF what-so-ever and his mind is filled with doubts. He is unsure of his future. He doesn't know mind power or the concept of 'follow your passion' or 'follow the process.' So there are too many distractions and even though the kid knows he is lacking behind in his performance, there is nothing much he can do about it. The 'Oh! so powerful' mind has a wilful mind of its own, and it just drifts away!

And there is nothing he can do about it.

That's because nobody had a chat with him about mental skills or awareness – the quintessential qualities that help you give your 100% to the job at hand. The numerous and ludicrous distractions make a monkey of the mind jumping, skipping and somersaulting everywhere at the same time, unable to keep it at one place for any length of time to make sense of it.

> "The format of the game is such that one extraordinary performance from one batsman from a side can tilt the game to their favour. So, I am not thinkingof the series finals. One match at a time. We walk into the field, give 100%, and then it's a fair game. It doesn't bother me."
> —MS DHONI after CSK's win against KKR, IPL 2015

The moment we train the brain to increase the awareness level, giving your 100%, when you wish to do so and in whatever job you wish to, it will become easy.

Once we know the concept and value of what Dhoni is saying here, it should become a habit. It should be systematically applied to all that we do and not just during selective occasions.

While we are dining or watching TV, the 100% concept doesn't really matter, but what matters is the constant practice of it and getting our mental score aligned to it in a fashion where giving 100% is not a matter of choice, but something that is a part of our attitude.

While talking to Dhoni's teachers, coaches, and friends I got to know that *this* attitude is Dhoni's key to success. No matter what game he played, he always gave his 100%. That may easily provoke us into asking whether Dhoni never thought of winning at all. Well, when he tells his teammates, 'Let's go, play the game, and win,' he is definitely thinking about winning. What he doesn't do is obsess about winning. There is a huge difference and knowing it defines his mental skills. Not obsessing about the final outcome, yet having the ability to give that 100% is not just a wise suggestion, it's mandatory. Obsessing about winning will never give you the desired result. There can never be any contradictory argument about it.

Obsessing also affects creativity. There are times, in every field of work or play, when a different take or angle or an innovative idea proves to be the winning point.

Like when Dhoni asked Indian bowler Ishant Sharma to throw bouncers because he is tall, and giving him his career best – 7/74, in a series against England in 2014.

A quick change of tactics brought in the desired result. And this kind of unconventional decision-making ability, like Dhoni's, is the outcome of a calm mind, which is not a wreck with negative thoughts. During such times a cool, calm mental state is paramount. A pressurized mind obsessing with just the end result can never be useful.

Dhoni is the Indian team's wicket keeper, who bats at number 7. But the range of records he holds proves that he has the ability to give his all.

And by now we probably know the reason.

He learnt the 'process' so well that he could bend the unwritten rules by staying within the rules. And to successfully twist a rule, one must actually learn it extremely well. Dhoni started playing cricket in the gullies of Ranchi with his friends and his passion made him sub-consciously follow the process. From the gullies, to the school team, to the club shuffle, to U-16, to U-19 and then to Team India, if anyone followed his journey, they will find that throughout the spread, Dhoni followed his 'giving 100%' and 'follow the process' principles meticulously.

Try it.

And for doing that you will not have to make frantic tours to Ranchi to hobnob with the captain. You just need to listen to him when he speaks in the media. There are only these few things really, that he talks about, when asked to comment about his skills and how he came so far. And what he says is not rocket science but simple everyday skills that every man knows but doesn't necessarily follow. And that's the trick, if one is listening with his awareness radar up.

Keep it simple!

While we are handpicking Dhoni's success *mantra* and dissecting it, Chapter 4 brings us to yet another of his pet phrase, which you can never miss if you are listening to him closely:

Carpe diem – Live in the moment!

The Crux

- **Simply keep executing step by step without giving too much thought and emotion to it.**

- **Follow the process, you will find results along the way.**

- **Keep fear, anger, and frustration away from your psychological orbit. They will destruct you.**

- **Obsession can take your energy and leave you nowhere. Stay calm and execute your process.**

- **Simple things always give the best results.**

FOUR

A Peaceful Walk Home!

> "You must live in the present, launch yourself on every wave, and find your eternity in each moment. Fools stand on their island of opportunities and look toward another land. There is no other land; there is no other life but this."
>
> —HENRY DAVID THOREAU

Here's taking a lesson from Bollywood, because we know how much we love to live in the world of films. In *Zindagi Na Milegi Dobara*, when the character of Hrithik Roshan, a financial broker, says to Katrina Kaif that since he enjoys cooking, he has this big plan of getting into it after he is 40-years-old. Kaif, cutting him short says, "Forty years is a long time". She continues by saying, "Seize the day my friend. First live this day to the fullest. Then plan for later."

Either victory or defeat, nothing seems to baffle Dhoni or excite him. He can leave victory like a thing of the past and move ahead like nothing happened. It looks like when he wins or loses, he tells himself: *this too shall pass.*

Living in the moment not only helps you get rid of the baggage, it also makes you free.

> "Staying in the moment is my mantra of success. I just go from one moment to another, that's the only thing in my head"
>
> —MS Dhoni

Dada reiterated the same thing. He said, "Sfurti, we all live in the present. We never think five months from now."

Like every Indian who swears by cricket, I too have been hooked to the game since I was 8 and had memorized the names of all the players of my country, Australia, England, New Zealand, and so on. The cricketing terms like 'square cut', 'over the boundary', and 'around the wicket' were no strangers to me and I could easily tell the difference between spinners and fast bowlers and could at any given time hold a respectable debate on cricket with elders over chai and *samosa*. But for me cricket always meant India, and it goes beyond saying that I didn't watch the matches in which India didn't play.

What is the point of carrying unnecessary baggage?

Then one day after a nail-biting, hair-raising finish between India and Pakistan, where India lost, my brother suddenly jumped up from the couch, threw his hands up and clapped aloud proclaiming over and again, "Oh, what a match! Oh, what a match!"

By then I was reduced to tears and could not fathom the reason behind his euphoria. When I looked at him, he said, "I know India lost, but it was a great match till the very last ball. Each and every player was so charged up. Did you see the expression on Shahid Afridi's face when he looked at Anil Kumble? Did you see how confident Rahul Dravid was when he hit those fours? Did you see Yuvi (Yuvraj Singh) rotating his shoulder? Gosh! That was such power display."

I was quiet for a moment. I realized that even though I sat tight for all those hours, I actually never noticed any of these! While he remembered each and every move that all the players made from both the teams, I remembered nothing except that India lost! What was I doing? Why can't I recall any of these things that my brother was talking about? I tried hard, but except for a few highlights of the day, I remembered nothing!

And I am sure you, my readers, are also not strangers to such a reaction.

I was too focussed on the outcome that I neither experienced nor enjoyed the 6-7 hours that I sat in front of the TV. I was just obsessed with the outcome, and hence, lost out on the moment.

Every event is the sum total of its moments. To live, is to be able to experience each of these moments – be it watching a match, first ball to the last, and enjoying each one of them irrespective of the end result; or playing it like Dhoni, who has mind-trained himself to treat each ball like a fresh one, each defeat a learning, and each game an experience, no matter what the result is. When you can do this it makes for a peaceful walk home.

Now, what do we mean by 'a peaceful walk home'?

To be present here and now, to be able to give your 100% and to experience it as a whole by not dividing the mind in several places, is my idea of a *peaceful walk home.* It's simply the ability to treat wherever you are at the moment as home.

To live in the moment means to unclutter the mind and to recognize the power of 'now'. Imagine walking back home after a hectic day and our mind is still clogged with the next day's itinerary. In our mind we are still processing the meetings, the files and the follow-ups, and in the process getting worked up about something that is happening the next day. If we live in the moment, this time of walking-back-home can be peaceful and relaxed. It can rejuvenate us and repair the psychological wear and tear. It can help us release stress, if only we can bring our mind to close the day and live the 'now' moment. But we usually don't. We are not off the hook. Instead we are in the waiting mode for the sun to rise so that we can get back again. But the trick lies here – to live in the moment and have a 'peaceful walk back home.'

Ask yourself this question when you are playing cricket, cooking, finishing your project, or tidying your wardrobe – is it a *peaceful walk back home?* Which means, '**is your mind there with your body or are you somewhere else?'**

> Life is what happens to you while you're busy making other plans.
>
> —JOHN LENNON

And that's what people usually do. Think about it? When they are physically somewhere, their mind is mostly somewhere else. People driving their car in the morning going to work, think about the meeting scheduled the first thing in the morning, a player practicing in the field thinks about victory, a housewife while cooking thinks about her free time, a working mother thinks about her baby when at work and worries about her work when at home. A person taking time off from work to relax hardly gets any because he is worried about the job at hand. A person sitting late night watching a match or catching up on a new Friday release worries about getting up late next morning. While biting into a juicy bit of cheese they worry about the amount of calories they are pumping in and working out in a gym is always a waste of time for it could have been used for something better.

Being mentally somewhere else is a negative psychological trait that hampers our growth. It affects our awareness ratio directly. Like this person, who is thinking about the scheduled meeting on his drive to work will definitely be thinking about the next meeting or the power point presentation that is scheduled later in the day while he is attending the meeting he was so worried about just a while back.

This person is constantly missing out on the 'now' moment. His walk back home is never peaceful.

> *No matter what you are doing, missing out on the 'now' moment grossly affects your productivity.*

To sportspersons of all genres, living in the moment is paramount to winning. No sportsman can ever win without this attribute. While in a team sport the phenomenon is not so obvious, in individual games it is very evident. The winner is always the person who can live in the moment.

You may have given a hundred wrong shots, but only the person who can 'live in the moment' is smart enough to believe that the next shot is going to be a killer making him win, just like Dhoni hits a six and finishes a match, and it's not without a reason that he is called the best finisher.

Lauding his talent, Ian Bishop, former West Indies cricketer and commentator, once said about Dhoni:

"If 15 runs are required off the last over,
pressure is on the bowler, not Dhoni."

Dhoni has proven himself to be the one who can turn a match around and bring home victory when others sitting in front of the TV have given up and are waiting for an inevitable loss. It's his supreme power of 'living in the moment' that enables him to do that. If we sift through his possible thought process at that moment, he must be calculating that what he needs is six runs from the next two balls and how he can get it. Any other thought falls outside the periphery. A winner's mind always lives in the moment.

Benefits of Living in the Moment

"I see pressure as an opportunity to do well. If you are under pressure you should not see it as a danger and give in to it."

—MS Dhoni

a. The Pink Crush

Expectation is pressure and a burden. Significantly so when you are captaining one of the best sides in the world and all eyes are hooked on you. Dhoni handles this pressure too well. It cannot be a burden to him. It is what that keeps him in demand. After listening to Dhoni,

I realized it's a **'pink-crush'**. For Dhoni, it makes him feel alive and wanted. It makes him feel important, and that whatever he does, say or think, matters to the world. For him, it's an opportunity to perform and re-establish to the world his 'hero' factor. And that's how he views pressure. For him it is a *'pink-crush'*. He has learned to take the pressure off the pressure and keep it in perspective.

"When I am batting, I focus on the ball. Sometimes my mind wanders off to places where it is not supposed to, but as soon as I notice it, I bring it back to the ball. Singing helps me to stay focused. When the bowler is running in to the crease, I start to sing but as soon as he gets to his delivery stride, I focus on the ball. Singing when the bowler is running in empties my mind of unwanted thoughts."

—MS DHONI (As quoted in *Think Like A Champion*)

He further added, "People say a lot of negative things about pressure. Pressure to me is just an added responsibility."

That is how I look at it: It's not pressure when God gives you an opportunity to be a hero for your team and your country.

If you expect pressure and have a plan to deal with it, you will know exactly what to do when it comes, and more often than not you will use it in a positive and productive way.

The best way to deal with it is to stay in the moment and not get trapped in the past or caught up in the future, or on what might happen in the end.

"If you stay in the moment, calm your mind and focus on the process you won't feel much pressure."

Dhoni has been a champion in handling pressure and whenever he is questioned how he does it, he always connects it with this 'living in the moment' concept. This 'pink-crush' approach to pressure is a **huge stress-buster.** If you can rule out impending deadlines, lurking criticism, possible failure, or a gloating success out of your mind by living in the moment and just concentrate on what is happening 'now', there is nothing much that can stop you from achieving your goal.

"One thing I like about him (Dhoni) is his calmness. I wish I could have some of it. He is someone who doesn't disclose too much which would let the opposition know about what's going on in his mind. I wish I could get some of it,"

—VIRAT KOHLI, Vice-captain & Captain, Indian Test Cricket Team.

Living in the moment spares enough mind space to make the right decisions. I like the word **'mind-space'** – the word is simple and yet impactful. The moment Dhoni says 'mind-space, you know that he is travelling without baggage in his mind. He has just packed in the required thoughts for the moment.

When India batsman Shikhar Dhawan was going through a bad phase, it was Dhoni who talked him out of it. After his smashing performance in the World Cup series of 2015, he had said that:

"The way Mahi *bhai* handled me and brought me out to this level is absolutely fantastic. He told me to keep doing what I do best – that is to play my cricket. 'You don't need to bother about other things as they are not in your control. Just live in the moment and follow the process. Focus.'"

b. Living in the moment makes you calm

Whether it was a terrific win or a bad loss, never has the commentary box stopped lauding Dhoni's super calm attitude and the title 'Captain Cool' has become a grand eponym for him. He says it is very important to stay in the present. It makes him calm and facilitates complete awareness on the field.

"For me every ball is a new opportunity,"

Dhoni said when asked how he could hit those record number of sixes in the last few overs to make the team win. And our captain always has his answers ready. Promptly he said he treats every game as a new game, likewise he treats every ball as a new ball. "Never mind if I have hit five dot balls in a row. The sixth ball is always a fresh ball and is full of possibilities," says Dhoni. The absolute 'now-moment' stress point gives him immense power and an edge over his opponents.

Even though people today know the value of this concept, very few practice it. Mind is a monkey refusing to stay put in a place for more than a few seconds. Try closing your eyes and concentrate on one particular thing – let's say a ball. You will find that keeping your thoughts around the ball for more than five seconds will be challenging. This exercise will give you an idea about how fretful the mind is and how important it is to tame it, achieve control over its fleeting nature, and then use it to your advantage. Therefore, this ability doesn't come in one day. One needs to practice it diligently in order to achieve that focus point. And when you reach that point where you can let go of the past and future and be in the 'now', things around you will start changing to your advantage.

For an international celebrity like Dhoni, where ten different things other than cricket demand his mind-space, living in the moment is an ultimate requirement.

We see him on the ground playing cricket, where he is the wicket-keeper, captain, and a batsman; we see him in TV commercials looking so handsome speeding a bike, mostly, or endorsing health drinks. Fans are crazy about him and girls would kill for that enamouring smile of his! He is surrounded by all these and yet his focus on his job never waivers.

"With all the adulation, how do you keep your feet on the ground?"

I asked him once. I was prepared for a long interview, but he was in a hurry and had asked me to walk along with him across the corridor. As we walked side by side I noticed that both the sides of the corridor were lined with fans fervently trying to steal a glimpse of their favourite hero. It was so picture perfect to walk along where he signed a few autographs, waved at his fans, smiled at the camera, and shook a few hands. I looked at him in awe as he handled the scenario so beautifully. I raised my eyebrow in awe and astonishment towards him and he smiled at me.

"I divide life into three lines, Sfurti. I have talked about this before as well. For me, **one is the praise line, the second is the criticism line, and the third is the straight line**. The straight line is the 'now' time. Like right now, I am talking to you. I stay on the straight line. People appreciate and criticize you. Neither should the praise go to your head nor do the criticisms bring you down. Just take the middle lane."

c. Let it flow

If you want my definition of Dhoni, then I would use a simile and call him a river. Because Dhoni never stops, struts, frets, or waits. He always flows, never stagnating at one place, and always unstoppable. For him the learning curve is unending. **To keep doing what you do is the**

motto. Happiness is not a name of a place where he needs to reach. Rather, it is a process. Every moment has a potential to make you happy, if you live in the moment and let everything else flow.

Dhoni says that he sings before he hits the ball to ward off negative thoughts and to empty his mind. When asked how is that negative thoughts doesn't cross his mind, he said that it definitely does.

> "Everyone has his share of negative thoughts. When there is a difficulty, I just switch off myself from the problem and do something absolutely different. Later, when I revisit the situation, I can easily find the solution. It comes fast. I believe that when there is a problem, there is always a solution. So I just leave it for some time and let it settle down."
>
> —MS DHONI

Now let me tell you something interesting about Dhoni. His favourite song is, "*Mein pal do pal ka shayar hoon/ Pal do pal meri kahani hai/Pal do pal meri hasti hai....*" Whenever he is asked to sing, this is probably the only song he hums. And if we follow the lyrics, it talks pretty much about 'living in the moment'!

Happiness happens to the one who truly knows how to live in the moment. Think of the time or the moment when you were really happy – an event maybe, or the company

> "I, not events, have the power to make me happy or unhappy today. I can choose which it shall be. Yesterday is dead, tomorrow hasn't arrived yet. I have just one day, today, and I'm going to be happy in it."
>
> —GROUCHO MARX

of a friend. That must have been the moment when you were 'present'. That must have been the moment when you neither thought of the past nor cared for the future. Those few moments were truly yours. That is living in the moment.

d. Multitasking

Dhoni is a three-in-one package – he bats, keeps wicket and takes catches, and he is also the captain of Team India. In one word, he's a multitasker. He is successfully gliding from one role to the other. High level of ability to live in the moment helps in the **switching on and switching off** concept. This increases our ability to **multitask.** Multitasking doesn't mean doing two or three jobs at the same time. Multitasking means the ability to switch on and switch off from one job to another in a smooth, seamless fashion that gives the onlooker an illusion that a person is handling multiple jobs at the same time. In fact, people who habitually multitask too think that they are handling multiple chores at one time. But they are actually switching from one task to another in matter of seconds.

If you place a glass of milk each next to two students who are studying and one of them drinks up his milk while the other doesn't, it does not mean that the student who drank his glass of milk is not focused in his studies, or that the student who forgot his milk is too much focused and engrossed in his studies. It simply means that the one who drank his milk is better at multitasking than the other.

I have often seen my mother talking over the cellphone clutched between her left ear and shoulder while she is packing my lunch, assisting me and my brother with our breakfast, and at the same time keeping an eye on the boiling milk pan on the stove.

She does that by successfully gliding from one role to another, and in that 15 seconds time concentrating fully on one task while the others take the back seat. She has mastered the art of multitasking like most mothers!

If we are committed to live in the moment in order to give our 100% we need to prioritize.

Prioritizing is a great tool to practice the above concept. Out of the 10 different things racing your mind, you prioritize what's most important, stay with it, and give it your undivided attention.

When I spoke to Dhoni, I asked him how he handled pressure, media criticism, expectations of an entire nation, friends, family and peers. He said:

"I prioritize and live with it. I will never be able to perform if I have all these things running through my mind. And the only way to get rid of them is to live in the moment. When I am in the field, cricket is my priority, not media, not fans or their criticism, or my family. That's the only way to perform and win."

How do we practice 'living in the moment'?

Although the concept of living in the moment is self-explanatory and we know what exactly we are supposed to do, doing it whatsoever needs practice. There are several ways to practice it, and meditation is very much advisable.

When I told Dhoni that 'living in the moment' is easier said than done, he said **"Today your life has 24 hours. Try respecting that. You will find the concept easy to adhere to."** Then he picked up a pen that was lying in the table at point A and asked me to place it at a certain point B. I did. He asked, "What did you just do?" I looked at him and said, "I moved the pen from here to there." "Exactly! Did you think about anything else? We need to cut down on unnecessary thinking and do what we need to do. That is living in the moment that I believe in," he said and smiled as he got up and walked out of the room.

It was about all the time he gave me that day, but the interaction was absolutely a knockout! I found the pen-

shifting process very interesting and easy to keep in mind. I loved the 24 hours count-down to life extremely powerful and therefor, I'm sharing it with you:

a. My 24-hours-of-life acknowledgement

You wake up in the morning and tell yourself that 24 hours is all that you have. And in each of that 24 hours there are as many as 60 minutes and in each of those 60 minutes there are 60 seconds. Tell yourself that each of those second is so precious to you and that you want to make them the most beautiful seconds of your life. You want to make them count.

The acknowledgement of this 24-hours-in-a-day concept first thing in the morning is a very powerful exercise and will go a long way to bring your focus right on the present moment every time you feel you are drifting away into a no man's land.

How does it work?

It trims down on your time management and helps flush out the garbage from your mind. What's left is pure and distilled. The outcome of it is stunningly fascinating.

24 × 60 × 60 Sec
Try and Respect
that!

Waking up when you acknowledge that 24 hours is all that you have in your day today, you automatically sift through the unwanted curriculum of our mind and focus on what you actually want to do and must be doing at this moment. You will, by default, avoid doing all those time-wasting activities like staring at the TV or spending too much time on the social network. This 24-hour concept helps us to value time, value ourselves, and live in the moment.

The 24-hours practice is a gem and I would suggest everyone to give it a shot. If Dhoni believes in it and likes to talk about it, I think it is worth giving it a shot.

I say it again.

Try toh karo!

b. Take time out to unwind

Dhoni's love for bikes is well known. He owns an enviable fleet of those beasts. Every time a reporter asks him about his bikes, his face lights up. When he is not playing cricket, he spends time with his bike, his dogs, playing football, spending time with family and friends. These days we see him a lot with his daughter Ziva, clinging to his chest.

When you take your mind and body out to unwind and relax, you are actually refuelling your system for better

> "I don't like to see the replay of a match. After a match is over, I don't like to discuss it either. I don't usually like talking about matches when we have free time or when we are relaxing."
>
> —MS DHONI

productivity. You might call it a 'strategic time-out'. During an event, Dhoni's colleague and eminent cricketer Virat Kohli too mentioned that their captain doesn't like dwelling on the match once it's over. There is a time assigned for such discussions where it's taken up in a constructive manner.

Unwinding is a crucial part. It refreshes the tired mind and helps us to live in the moment in a fresh, energized manner. Doing a job for too long without any rest has adverse effects on our nervous system. The signals sent across by a tired neurological system are not always up to the mark. Trying to give a job your 100% with a tired mind does not yield the desired result. Focus does not mean you have to be at it 24/7. Doing so makes the fizz escape. It catches up on you in the wrong way. No matter how dear the job is for you, 24/7 schedules will wear you out, leading to exhaustion and thereby resulting in disinterest. This will make you lose focus on your job.

c. Maintain a blue board

Make it pink or even green if you like (it's a beautiful colour by the way). But try this strategy:

A blue board is a physical graph that you chalk out and pin it on a board where you can see it easily. It may be in your kitchen, in your bedroom, or on the soft board on your office desk. The graph records time against achievements with a goal set right on top and small mid-term goals along its path.

It sharpens the focus and keeps you on track because you can actually see the goalpost!

One sweet spot of this graph is that once you have written down the goal, which is the end result of all the effort that you are going to put in, you can let it go out of your active mind. It's out on the board for you to see, so you don't have to clog your brain with it. It's vital for the concept of 'live in the moment and not to worry about the result' part. You can then tune yourself into the process of giving your 100% to the small targets you have set for yourself. Achieving those small, set targets keeps you motivated every time you are able to put a tick mark against it. It keeps you in the positive frame of mind since you are achieving something, you are making progress, and you can calculate it on the blue board.

Try it once at least just for the sake of testing it, like when you are trying to lose weight, or learn swimming, or win a game of chess with your chess-veteran dad. It works every time. The only condition is that the board needs to be kept somewhere where you can always see it!

This concept not only allows you to give 100% to your job but also increases your awareness level. The blue board keeps you in the moment and frees you from anxiety, fear, and all such emotions that are commonly associated with linked-memory. A person who has experienced this has affirmed to an amazing experience.

Before I end this chapter, I would like to pen down an interesting observation. 'Living in the moment' is a catchy phrase and has got a cool quotient to it, so much so that people like to use it on the fly for all the wrong reasons and with the wrong attitude. Like wasting all the valuable time in mindless merriment with no thought what so ever of the future, or throwing away money in vain thinking that this is what is called 'living in the moment'.

But I have seen Dhoni use this concept to pave his path towards success. He wrung out the real meaning of it and used it to his betterment. He chiselled it through the years till the skill itself made a gem out of him. Today, MS Dhoni is not just a cricketer, but a cricketer with a difference, who is talked about and discussed not just in the commentary box, but outside the realms of cricket, even in corporate board rooms! And if that is not enough, Dhoni's leadership skills is studied in B-schools across the globe and aspiring leaders of all genre are trying to imbibe his success mantras to push ahead in life.

THE CRUX

- **Living in the moment and attacking each second to the fullest is the greatest secret of being productive.**

- **Being in the present keeps you away from the past which is useless and future which will be created to your present. Present must be good to have an excellent future.**

- **'My 24-hours' is one of the best practices I have ever come across. In those 24 × 60 × 60 seconds, try and smile all the time.**

- Keep calm. The person who can't keep calm is a useless commodity in crises.

- You and not the situation should have the power to control your emotions. Make yourself that strong.

FIVE

To Be the Chosen Leader

"He is a great leader by example, someone whom I have always admired for his ability to remain balanced and has the sense of equanimity about his captaincy."

—RAHUL DRAVID

"If I am to select a team, Sachin will be the opener and Dhoni the captain."

—STEVE WAUGH

"As far as ODI is concerned, Dhoni is one of the greatest captains of all times in India."

—SOURAV GANGULY

The above quotes from cricketing stalwarts establish that Dhoni is not just a selected captain of Team India, he is the chosen leader. The uniqueness of his leadership skills is the talk of the town. People around the world are enthralled by his leadership skills. I thought it might be worthwhile to fish for a few takeaways on this aspect.

So, what are the takeaways?

Dhoni's people management skills

The foremost quality of a leader is the way he manages his men. Whether it was backing newcomers like Shikhar Dhawan and Rohit Sharma or letting his teammates bask in the glory of the 2011 World Cup victory, MS Dhoni believes in giving importance to the team and space to his players. This ambience provided by the captain gives a sense of freedom to the teammates thereby empowering them. He practically handed over the 2011 World Cup victory moment to Sachin Tendulkar and walked away. When Sourav Ganguly was playing his last Test match at Nagpur, Dhoni made him the captain of the Team for some time as a tribute to the icon.

During an IPL match in Hyderabad, the Chennai Super Kings (CSK) team was put up in a five-star hotel. Local player Ambati Rayudu's family had delivered some home cooked biryani for the team at the hotel. But the hotel staff refused to let the team have it sighting that outside food was not allowed inside. Dhoni found the incident so humiliating that he and the entire CSK team walked out and promptly checked into another five-star. Debasish

Dutta said that the food was not the point. The disrespect towards the effort of his teammate and his family was what triggered the reaction.

As a leader, to know your people beyond their required skills for the job is a very important attribute. Dhoni knows his people and is attached to their emotions. He respects them, stands by them, and fights for them.

Dhoni's leadership style gives a stiff competition to bossiness where members are simply expected to listen and obey. Dhoni is not a boss. He is a leader who allows his team think, feel the right and wrong in every situation and then take solution-based decisions, which enable best results in every task at hand, says Vandana Shah, executive and leadership coach at The Chrysallis. "The difference between a boss and a leader is that a boss dictates terms, while a leader like Dhoni develops the team members, such that there is no more need for a system to follow or enforce, but where members work in sync on their own."

Being flexible to the development of team members also helps them evolve and build their emotional stability. While we all know the importance of the strength of mind to win, Dhoni is perhaps the only person who knows how far emotional stability goes hand in hand with winning. If we talk to his teammates, we get to know that this is one area Dhoni works on with his team members. The rest automatically falls in place.

He follows some core values

Dhoni is **trustworthy**. When he enters the field with a bat, he wins. It's seldom that the team lost with Dhoni on the crease. That is his trademark. It has become a belief that if the opposition cannot get him out, they cannot win. This character trait of Dhoni – being trustworthy has been tapped by a lot of brands to which he is a brand ambassador. When Dhoni endorses a brand people believe in it. Today this very trait makes him one of the richest athletes in the world.

He **stands by** his teammates. Cricketer Mohammad Shami says today he is a good bowler only because Dhoni stood by him in his difficult times. He has never put his teammates down. Shikhar Dhawan too attributes his success to Dhoni's captaincy. Whenever Dhoni is asked to comment on a bowler who did badly during a match, he always takes his bowler's side and says that such thing happens in a match.

Even though Dhoni is known as a man of few words, he is never shy of expressing himself. It is very interesting to see that a man like him, who is generally known to be a quiet person, knows exactly what to say when it comes to real issues and the need to express views, which again is a very essential quality of a leader. Nobody likes a loud leader, but everybody looks forward to the one who can guide them in the right direction and is not afraid to do so.

A leader cannot be a 'YES MAN'. He knows he cannot

make everyone happy all the time. Dhoni prefers to keep his team close and protect it even if it means standing against the world.

He is a leader who **leads from the front.** Rahul Dravid said, "Dhoni has never demanded anything from his teammates which he himself has never done. Dhoni is one leader who leads through example, not by rhetoric."

Dhoni is **honest.** And that itself is one quality that has seen him climb those mountains of success. In an interview Dhoni once said that even if he is a celebrity, he would want the world to remember him just as a 'good-man'. While this statement might come across as fancy, we have found that Dhoni has displayed this very quality many a times on the field. For example, in 2011, when India was on a tour of England, Ian Bell was declared run out on the on-going second test. The ball rolled to the boundary and Bell thought he had hit a four. He walked off the crease only to be run out by Dhoni. The Indian side of course appealed and Bell was given out. But Dhoni withdrew his appeal as a display of his sportsman spirit and called Bell to continue. Bell at that moment was playing at 163 and he was a crucial batsman for the England line-up.

All these attributes, though sounds simple, gives Dhoni the uncanny edge over the others. It is said that he is not as skilled as Dravid, Sachin, Ganguly, or Adam Gilchrist. Yet, he is the best.

The world witnessed not just a winner, but the onset of a natural leader with some noticeable and rare leadership qualities. His extraordinary ability to **read the game** has been crucial in many wins. With World Twenty20, the Commonwealth Bank series, the Border-Gavaskar trophy, ICC World Cup, and the Champions Trophy, all under his belt, he has led Indian cricket to scale loftier heights than any captain had ever done before him.

A Natural Leader

We have witnessed captains like Sourav Ganguly, Mohammad Azharuddin, and Steve Waugh, among many others. Yet the world calls Dhoni the 'natural leader'.

It's his perspective and approach to the job. And why do I call it a job right now and not just the game of cricket? Because here I am drawing a parallel to his skill set as a leader that applies to all aspiring leaders in any given field.

No one understands it better than him that when the method is followed, sooner or later victory is evident.

Management gurus commented that his skill sets as a leader are the kinds that are taught in high management schools. He applies them in a manner as if he has graduated from one of the best finishing school of management that's there in the world. He is a natural when it comes to being a leader.

When one looks at Dhoni and the way he conducts himself on the field and off the field, his offbeat style of captaincy, his wins and losses, one gets a sense of completeness or wholesomeness about his persona. And this is one vital aspect of a good leader – a leader exudes a sense of wholesomeness. A leader should not only bring in laurels, but should also be trusted by his teammates. His honesty should lead the way and his values should be such that people around learn from it.

Best Finisher

Dhoni's glamorous attribute to the game is that he is an excellent finisher. Sachin, during the last IPL, commenting on Dhoni, said, "The best thing about Dhoni is that he is a great finisher. It is not how you begin but how one finishes. Dhoni is one of the few people who know how to do so.'

Most people start something, but somewhere in between they lose steam. People have the tendency to lose focus and consistency in the middle of a job. For example, winning the first match and losing remaining of the matches in the series. Or, writing the first paper well and ignoring the rest. The magnanimous ways in which Dhoni has finished games, and led the Team to a win in tight circumstances has brought to limelight the very concept of the importance of being a finisher and the skill sets required to be so.

> *"It's not how well you begin, but how beautifully you finish a job decides a winner."*

What does being a good finisher mean?
Everything in life has a beginning and an end. It is

important for an individual to recognise the end point taking from the start and finish it successfully. What does recognising the end point mean?

For a person who is good in studies, it is not only important to score high marks academically and acquire multifarious degrees, his main aim should be to reach the end drawing a finishing line to the job at hand.

For a person who is a good dancer, sportsman or a singer, it is important for them to not only hone their skills and do it well, but to do everything that is required in order to take your skill set to its destination.

Likewise, if I am considering myself a good writer simply because I write well it will not do me any good to jam my laptop with files showcasing my writing skills. That's just the beginning of a process. I would carry my dream to a destiny when I give my writing a form and approach the publishers, market it till I get what I desired.

To talk about the man, who for the world is a living example of calmness and quick decision making, Dhoni doesn't just mean playing cricket or a certain captaincy. He is God when it comes to handling pressure. If his start was his passion for cricket, his end point is his ability to take his passion to the highest level, to put in the required effort to place it in the right forum, to make his passion earn riches and respect for him, to get the full out of it. Only then his job is done.

When opponents, cricket fans and analysts witness Dhoni's captaincy on the field, they are treated to a mixture of **strength, simplicity and calmness.** Rahul Dravid, too commented on Dhoni's remarkable ability to soak in pressure. He said that in a team game, this attribute goes a long way in becoming a successful and functional leader. In his long stint in the field, Rahul Dravid says that, of all the players, national and international, that he encountered, this quality of Dhoni makes him 'Standout'. *It was Sachin Tendulkar who suggested his name for captaincy saying, "Give Dhoni the opportunity. He has excellent relation with his teammates. He will know how to handle the team." Under Dhoni's captaincy we won the world cup.*

The quintessential attributes of a leader in any aspect of life are – a spin-off thought process, backing team members at all cost, motivating them on and off the field, handling pressure and keeping things simple.

Dhoni is known for this emotional balance. No matter what the situation is, he keeps it well under control. He is aware of the spotlight but never hogs the limelight.

In a hierarchy driven society Dhoni was made the Captain ahead of several senior players. He played captain to Sachin Tendulkar, Sourav Ganguly and Rahul Dravid.

In any organisation, leadership qualities or its acknowledgement is not confined to the time spent in the organisation. Leadership trait in a person is independent of all these factors. Dhoni did not have to spend a stipulated time there to qualify as a captain. His leadership skills were good enough for him to qualify. Similarly these days, you don't have to spend five years to get into a leadership role. Displaying your leadership qualities will itself take you places.

Leadership is a complete mental skill – part natural, part acquired or achieved. Even in a hierarchy set up, it has been seen that people who can successfully display leadership traits have broken the hierarchical ladder and stepped ahead.

To achieve leadership skills, first it is important to know what these skills are. What is expected of a leader? Who is a leader? What are its values?

A leader is a person who has the capability to see much ahead of the ongoing game. He is the only person in the group, who can see beyond the set rules and regulations, question norms and practices and be cool enough to change a few. A leader is a person who leaves his signature in the job.

When Dhoni talks about his take on the game we see a distinct leader speak. He made the game better by simply 'simplifying' it, when there was a fast track method in place complicating it more and more as days went by. He redefined aggression by simply not being aggressive and addressed hostility by refusing to give in to it.

Today there is a distinct Dhoni-style cricket to be seen. It is widely believed by the cricketing fraternity in particular and experts at large that when Dhoni leaves the game he will leave the game better. The game itself will be promoted to the next level. Cricket today already talks about two different eras – cricket pre-Dhoni and cricket post Dhoni. They talk about something called the 'Dhoni-style' of cricket. We also hear about 'untutored-style' VS cricketing academy style, post Dhoni. Commentators talk about Dhoni's 'rugged' approach to the gentleman's game. And all these became possible after a certain boy from Ranchi made it possible for himself for the world to make cricketing terms on him. And this, my Dear Readers, is a massive take away for me from Dhoni. When all the mental skills that we talked about in this book are incorporated within our persona, we get to leave a mark, our own signature mark to the job we undertake.

It's no less an achievement for Dhoni that if today little children from small towns dare to dream and make it big, Dhoni and his massive success has got a great deal to do with it. And if your deeds are great enough to inspire kids and show them the way, then you are a leader!

One of the greatest strength of a leader is that he accepts himself as a leader. He is not afraid to step-up and stand in-front of the herd when called upon.

Most so called leaders, especially in the corporate world or a self-founded business finds themselves in a leadership position by virtue of promotion or ownership. Not all of them necessarily possess leadership skills or values. Almost all of them lack distinct vision. And none whatsoever has any real clarity

> If you are a lion, call yourself a lion

on the concept of it. When they are faced with a hurdle, they quickly search for a shoulder to put the blame on.

The result?

Of all businesses, 87.32% fail in the first three years of starting. The owner gropes in the dark but fails to understand the reason behind the failure. He sees the money invested, the strategic location, the planning, and the resource. But he fails to foresee the need of a leader. He is no visionary. He has no idea of the concept.

On the other hand, most corporate leaders are essentially managers in their function. They just have more responsibilities and probably a set of people to please. As a leader they just manage people and manage business. Very few think in terms of making a difference or bringing in a change even though huge amount of funds, resources and power are vested in him by virtue of his position. I have found that almost all of them are consumed with fear of failure. Their fear paralyses any new thought process, and in the end they land up just running the show just the way it was. They exit without creating any ripples or ruffling any feathers. Vice presidents, senior vice presidents, CEOs and CFOs are found in dozens and scores that pebble an organisation. But how many have we ever heard of? Very few. And we probably heard about those few of them because they somehow made a difference, stood up when required and led the pack. They were those people who were not afraid to call themselves the Lion.

Leadership is a unique attribute and the recognition of it must come early on in life. One needs to identify those traits within themselves.

A leader can handle criticism

This is one of the biggest traits of a leader. Dhoni was heard saying that he takes criticism into his stride and works on it. He never tries to negate a criticism but annihilates it. A leader is not afraid of criticism. He knows that when he is trying to do something different it is bound to face opposition. It's part of the game. Be it cricket or corporate. Until an effort is transformed into something new and shows positive result the world criticises a new introduction. But not giving up is what shapes a leader.

A leader is also a person who has *trained his brain to keep it free* from worries. We all will counter that worrying from time to time is given. Probably yes. But people, who give in to worry, seldom make a leader. It is not always that he knows that there is victory at the end of the road. But what he knows is that as long as he does not give up at the first sign of failure, he will see victory at the end of the tunnel.

A leader knows the *value of team work*. Dhoni swears by it. He seldom attributes victory to himself. He always talks about the boys who contribute. It is paramount to acknowledge that no matter how great a leader you are, you are ultimately nothing without your team.

He is a great communicator

When Dhoni speaks, the entire cricketing world listens, so do the common people. Kids from small towns, who too have a dream, listen. People from all walks of life, a beginner, big corporate honchos and motivational gurus listen to that one man who has changed the face of world cricket. And probably you, my readers, if you haven't done that already, will also listen and that's why this book. ***A great motivator***. He knows exactly how to bring the entire Team into one platform. Some touching success stories amongst the new comers in the Team is dedicated to Dhoni He motivates them in such a manner that they are able to discover their higher self. It is an interesting observation that post match, when the players are interviewed, they tend to speak the same language – 'I am trying to live in the moment,' 'give my 100%', 'trying to follow the process', etc., which is typically Dhoni mantra. He has practically dug these mantras into them.

So what makes Dhoni a successful Leader?

His lion attitude which has sailed him through everything mattered. He stood up to the moment, and accepted the leader in him very smoothly. The presence of giants like Sachin, Dravid and Ganguly did not scare him. Neither did the idea of captaining them scandalize him. He went along just being himself and allowed the natural leader in him to flourish. He talked to Ganguly about his rank in the batting line up. He debated Sachin on field strategy. He discussed stuff with Dravid. He took advice from everyone. He never missed an opportunity to learn. And that is one of his greatest attributes. Once when he was asked about how he feels being a captain to Ganguly and Sachin Tendulkar, he responded by saying that when he is in the field he

> *"does not see them as the-icon-Sourav Ganguly or the-icon-Sachin but just as a teammate whom he needs to captain".*

He is fearless. He can take calculated risks, like, tampering with the set batting order or choosing a bowler. When he wins, he does so without much fanfare and he loses without regret. Even as he makes the call in the field, his decision comes under great scrutiny. We hear them all too clear from the commentary box. But he is one captain who does not think of consequences. He plays by his gut feeling, and more often than not it has paid off.

Today I am a motivational speaker.

And I have a vision.

My vision is to bring people in touch with their dreams and aspirations. To create a bridge between happiness and success in every budding mind, to make people aware that prosperity comes from a happy state of mind and so does the coveted car. The importance of giving your 100% for

your dream is not a dream if you do not have the courage or the passion to chase it. And to talk passion and put it in the dictionary of every growing mind so that every output of every mind is unique. I want to be there with you as you discover the uniqueness in yourself, for nature made each one of us unique. It's the time in between that I will want to bridge and see the beauty of it as it unravels. I have my passion and I am on it, chasing it with all I have.

So, dear readers, what is your vision?

The Finish

> "It's a funny thing about life –
>   If you refuse to accept
> Anything but the best,
>   You very often get it!"
>   — By W. SOMERSET MAUGHAM

Terminating my journey here, yet not quite ending it, as it again is a process, if I am asked to sum up the whole book in just one line, I would say – "You just have one life. Learn to make it worthwhile."

In the beginning of the book I asked myself as to why I qualify to write a book on Dhoni, or for that matter, any great personality?

The answer was simple

As a little girl, like all the other girls, I grew up admiring them. My friends at one point thought I was out of my mind; after all, there are very few 'sports-crazy' girls. My parents were worried about me. They thought all I would do my entire life is to madly love celebs. But it was not that. I did not paint things red. I instead learnt from them. I tried to find out what made them great. What was common among these great people? What was it that separated great men from average ones and successful ones, and also good ones?

And finally, can I be one of them?

I picked up Dhoni because I am him. When I see him, just him the person and not the cricketer, I can identify myself with him. I too belong to a small town with a regular background and big dreams. If he is talented in sports, I too have my cache of talents. But he is big. He is an international celebrity. And I want to be him. I have learnt that if he can, I too can. I learnt it from him that dreaming big in not being foolish. 'Being practical in life' does not mean doing what thousand other people do – become a doctor, engineer or a chartered accountant. Being practical means doing exactly what your heart desires. It means doing it the right way, giving it that finish of perfection that leaves a mark, a signature. Giving it all you have and then some more. Being practical means pursuing your dream with a fiery passion and belief. Make it run in your body like hot blood. Then, only then will it become great and do all great things for you.

These days when I see all these talent hunt shows

on television, I am dumbstruck with the bulk of talents youngsters of this country has. Or even the world for that matter. But all of them are not successful. That's because they do not have the knowledge or awareness of mental skills. I want each and every kid, above the age of 14 to read this book so that they understand the power of their mind. So that they know that if their dreams do not, so to say, fall-in-line with the commoners, there is nothing wrong in it. All of them need to know that faith, hope and dream are for real. As real as Dhoni who came from a humble background and went on to become an international celebrity.

I want all young moms to read this book so that they can desist from trying to squeeze in their little ones into the standard pipeline of perceived success and let them dream.

I want every person, who thinks themselves a failure in life, to read this book, because there is nothing called failure. There is just giving-up.

I want all those people, who are not crazy enough to dream, to read this book. For what is life, if there is not a little passion and space enough to be a little crazy!

All great people believed in their passion and lived their dreams by treading into the path of their passion loaded with mental skills. They welcomed change. They understood the importance of it. This book and all other books that talk about winners will be of no use if the "YOU" in it is not open to bring about these changes. These knowledge would be absolutely fascinating and absolutely useless if "YOU" do not put in the effort to use them.

The study of mental skills and their benefits are not some inventions of a science laboratory. They have been galvanized through centuries by studying these very great people who stood apart. These skills are pure distillations of their winning mind. Hence the conclusion, that every person has the capability of being someone extraordinary by using these defined mental skills.

So usher in change. Nobody is born perfect. And nobody needs to die imperfect.

Dhoni has taught me never to settle for the second best. It doesn't work. People who excel never settle for the second best. Those who settle for the second best never excel. It is as simple as that. It never varies. The world is beaded with people who settle for the second best. Kill their heart and get along. Pay their bills. But to get exactly what you want, needs perseverance, a bend of mind that people call eccentric. Like Thomas Alva Edison, whose invention of the electric bulb required as many as 1000 experiments and that many number of failures. Like Neil Armstrong who was eccentric enough to dream of stepping on the moon. Like the Wright Brothers who were crazy enough to believe that man can fly or Dhoni, who ever thought of playing besides the biggies even as he worked in the Indian Railways and played cricket in the alleys with a canvas ball.

The trick is to never give up, because that's not the definition of success.

Be yourself

Realize the power of being yourself. Be unique. Dhoni doesn't or hasn't imitated anyone, in fact he has carved out a niche for himself through his trademark persona which today has become synonymous with him. The world hails him for this originality.

Our point is very simple.

Realize your own dreams than trying to live in others'. Don't try to imitate someone else, no matter how great he or she is.

Don't follow others blindly or try to trace their steps, no matter how divine those steps are.

Don't be someone else's great, because it will never be your great.

Your dreams are your own and you are your own judge. Be wise. Be aware of the existence of the mental skills and scaffold your dreams with them.

Do not ignore the journey of your goal to your success. The trick to understand is that the realization of success does not lie at your destination, but in the journey itself. Don't miss out on it.

If we are listening, all big people talked about the importance of the journey and never tried to surpass it. All the books that I have read about achievers across the globe, have mentioned in length the importance of experiencing the journey in the way to success. And once they completed the journey they confirmed it several times over that everything comes from all these unbelievable beautiful words like 'enjoying life', 'live-in-the-moment', 'be happy,' and 'follow your dreams.' These are the crux to living, success and greatness. The ones who understood the wisdom of it have discovered the opportunity to live the life of fulfilment. The rest spend a lifetime to come by this shell of wisdom. So it's often too late. And the result – too little.

Don't give a half-hearted effort. Charge on, for the world is too vast and life too short. Dreams must come true. Open your mind and understand the vastness of it. It's as huge as the ocean and it does not shore. This, again, is not something I am claiming or displaying, like my power of power-speech. Great men like Einstein, Michelangelo and Socrates have said it, and proved it with their very existence and extra-ordinary achievements. I am just rephrasing it for your benefit.

In the end why choose Dhoni? is the answer to the youth of this country and world as a whole. If kids from small unheard towns and villages are daring to dream big, then Dhoni has a great role to play in it. And this is the spirit that I want to bring forth through this book. He is there, right in front of us. Look at him. Study him. Listen to him when he speaks and hear him say, in very simple words, the basic **mantra** of life. Learn the art of winning. He gives them in droplets of manna dews. Soak them in.